Book content

PROLOGUE
How to develop our personality!

Continuous development of our personality as long as we live is absolutely necesary and this must be one of our personal permanent purpose.

Continuous development of our personality helps us a lot:

1. To achieve a happy and successful life
2. To form and develop more qualities, abilities, capacities, positive and efficient behavior.
3. To prevent mistakes, faileurs and errors
4. To find the right life partener
5. To find and maintain a happy marriage
6. To increase very much our chances to succed in life
7. To find more opportunities and lucks.
8. To raise better our children
9. To accomplish more of our personal objectives.
10. To find and maintain easier the jobs that we want.
11. To accomplish more in life.

12. To increase our self confidence and the power to succeed in our personal objectives.
13. To increase constantly our personal power
14. To become more popular and credible
15. To make our life more beautiful, pleaent and fulfilled.
16. To settle and accomplish more and more higher personal objectives.

We must form, develop and continously maintain the desire of super develop our personality. Continously we must set more time, energy, money and resources in our personal development to achieve a personal super development of our personality.

Personal super development increases more our chances to accomplish more and more in life.

Using the ideas form this volume and the ones succeding this and put into practise will certanly contribue to the development of our personality and to the accomplish of all that we want.

This volumes must be bought and used day by day, in order to development your personality and to the accomplish of all that you want.

The banking investent in this book of mine and the others that follow it is worth it, and it is almost nothing comparing to the pozitive efects that this book can have in your life. These books contain lots of pozitive, optimist, creative, dinamic ideas, that push you to action, to thinking, things that are necesary your daily life and to accomplish your personal objectives.

Some of the ideas we might all know but when we need them mostly (in griefs, faileurs, when we want to have a solution to our problems), we don't remember them to help us when we need.

That's why it is necessary to have them organized in books and in need to read them.

Reading and analizing the ideas in this book and aplying them, we'll fiind solutions and ideas that will help us find:

I. To discover:

    1. qualities
    2. defects
    3. capabilities

4. qualifications
5. some opportunities to succeed in life
6. feelings
7. what we do to be loved
8. how to love
9. how to realize and maintain a true mutual love
10. how to realize and maintain a happy marriage
11. mistakes, errors, wrong ideas
12. etc.

II. To prevent some:
1. divorces
2. mistakes
3. suspect
4. griefs
5. conflicts
6. accidents
7. failures
8. bankrupstcy
9. etc.

III. To become more:
1. happy
2. loved
3. honored,
4. appreciated,

5. wanted,
6. optimistic,
7. good,
8. unselfish,
9. emotional,
10. altruists
11. stronger
12. efficient
13. organized
14. planners
15. active
16. honest
17. human
18. popular
19. famous
20. flexible
21. adaptable
22. understanding
23. prompt
24. etc.

IV. To get out of a state of:
1. despair
2. pessimism
3. passiveness
4. inactivity
5. inefficiency
6. inflexibility
7. crisis

8. inadaptability
9. etc.

V. To participate more actively to:

1. social life
2. political life
3. nonprofit organizations activities
4. etc

VI. To participate more actively and efficiently in achieving true love and a happy marriage

VII. To find more likely situations conducive to achieving and maintaining a happy marriage life

VIII. To change our life for the better and to make it more beautiful

IX. To multiply and increase the chances to find your life partner

X. To raise and educate our children better so we can take better care of them

XI. Fiind more and bigger chances to meet favourable situations to accomplish and maintain a happy marriage for life.

XII. Change our life in good and make it better.

XIII. To multiply and increase the chances to find your life partner

XIV. To raise and educate our children better so we can take better care of them

I write and gather these thoughts, ideas in books, internet and other publications because these are useful to us every day and it is necessary to apply them to accomplish what we want, a better and beautiful life and propsperous.

These thoughts reflect a small part of what is good in reality and human relationships.

I wait to hear from you good news, good deeds that you have done influenced from what you have read from these books to make your life more beautiful, properous, happier and to be a pozitive example for others.

Each of us an become pozitive examples for others around us, participating to the creation of a better, prosperous and happier human society.

I'd be happy if one or more ideas read from these books helped you in a way or another and made you happier and prosperous.

I'm waiting to hear from you, your ideas and oppinions, your joys and griefes and your suggestions for new book subjects and i also appeal to your participation of promoting on the internet and mass media of the ideas and the books i've written.

I invite you to e-mail me at my email address: agcornel@gmail.com.

Dear readers I wish you all health, happiness and achievement of all your wishes.

Best regards and respect,

Ardelean Gheorghe Cornel

981 Principal Street
Macea, county Arad
Zip Code 371210
Romania
Tel # (40)-0788-725-204
(40)-0788-725-913

Abilities

1. A great capacity of using abilities must be maintained.

2. A great capacity of using abilities helps us maintain our happiness.

3. A great capacity of using abilities helps us achieve more favorable chances.

4. A great capacity of using abilities helps us become humane.

5. A great capacity of using abilities helps us maintain our optimism.

6. A great capacity of using abilities helps us achieve more efficient co operations.

7. A great capacity of using abilities helps us maintain our way of being loving.

8. A great capacity of using abilities helps us become more efficient.

9. A great capacity of using abilities helps us become cautious.

10. A great capacity of using abilities helps us become more cautious.

11. A great capacity of using abilities helps us become more productive.

12. A great capacity of using abilities must be rewarded.

13. A great capacity of using abilities must be imitated.

14. A great capacity of using abilities helps us become more enthusiastic.

15. A great capacity of using abilities helps us become more loved.

16. A great capacity of using abilities helps us maintain our way of being liked.

17. A great capacity of using abilities must be used.

18. A great capacity of using abilities helps us become enthusiastic.

19. A great capacity of using abilities helps us become more humane.

20. A great capacity of using abilities must be developed.

21. A great capacity of using abilities helps us become more loving.

22. A great capacity of using abilities helps us maintain our humanity.

23. A great capacity of using abilities helps us maintain our enthusiasm.

24. A great capacity of using abilities helps us become more tolerant.

25. A great capacity of using abilities must be appreciated.

26. A great capacity of using abilities helps us become loved.

27. By developing their inner beauty, women also develop their abilities that can help them achieve raising their children well.

28. By developing their inner beauty, women also develop their abilities of that can help them achieve efficient co operations.

29. By developing their inner beauty, women also develop their abilities that can help them achieve understanding in marriage.

30. By developing their inner beauty, women also develop their abilities that can help them achieve true friends.

31. By developing their inner beauty, women also develop their abilities that can help them achieve harmony in their marriage.

32. By developing their inner beauty, women also develop their abilities that can help them prevent certain misunderstandings.

33. The abilities that we need including those to achieve personal goals can be formed, developed, maintained and used through the contribution of the formation, development, maintenance and usage of the ability to find solutions to problems we want to solve.

34. Abilities can be formed through positive behaviors.

35. Abilities can be formed through prevision.

36. Abilities can be developed also through using efficient behaviors.

37. Abilities can be developed also through using efficient and behaviors.

Accomplish

38. The desire to accomplish records helps us achieve more efficient co operations.

39. The passion of accomplishing successes helps us achieve more favorable situations.

40. The ability to accomplish personal objectives helps us achieve more records.

41. We can contribute to the achievement of our greatest accomplishments also through the contribution of the formation, development, maintenance and usage of reserved behavior.

42. We can contribute to the achievement of our greatest accomplishments also through the contribution of the formation, development, maintenance and usage of fighting behavior.

43. We can contribute to the achievement of our greatest accomplishments also through the contribution of the formation, development, maintenance and usage of funny behavior.

44. We can contribute to the achievement of our greatest accomplishments also through the contribution of the formation, development, maintenance and usage of being a good listener behavior.

45. We can contribute to the achievement of our greatest accomplishments also through the contribution of the formation, development, maintenance and usage of energetic behavior.

46. We can contribute to the achievement of our greatest accomplishments also through the contribution of the formation, development, maintenance and usage of joyful behavior.

47. We can contribute to the achievement of our greatest accomplishments also through the contribution of the formation, development, maintenance and usage of continuous efficient usage of our time.

48. A great capacity of accomplishing strategies of applying thinking on a big scale must be a model.

49. We can contribute to the achievement of our greatest accomplishments also through the contribution of the formation, development, maintenance and usage of continuous self-control behavior.

50. We can contribute to the achievement of our greatest accomplishments also through the contribution of the formation, development, maintenance and usage of inventive behavior.

51. A great capacity of accomplishing strategies of applying thinking on a big scale helps us become more efficient.

52. A great capacity of accomplishing strategies of applying thinking on a big scale helps us maintain our enthusiasm.

53. We can contribute to the achievement of our greatest accomplishments also through the contribution of the formation, development, maintenance and usage of continuous self-motivating behavior.

54. We can contribute to the achievement of our greatest accomplishments also through the contribution of the formation, development,

maintenance and usage of expansive behavior.

55. A great capacity of accomplishing strategies of applying thinking on a big scale helps us achieve more favorable chances.

56. A great capacity of accomplishing strategies of applying thinking on a big scale helps us achieve more true friendships.

57. We can contribute to the achievement of our greatest accomplishments also through the contribution of the formation, development, maintenance and usage of sociable behavior.

58. We can contribute to the achievement of our greatest accomplishments also through the contribution of the formation, development, maintenance and usage of unpretentious behavior.

Achieve

59. The ability to ignore the word NO helps us achieve more pleasant surprises.

60. The ability to ignore the word NO helps us achieve more favorable chances.

61. The art of solving disagreements helps us achieve more successes.

62. Persevering in not letting ourselves be stopped helps us achieve more records.

63. Preventing the inefficient use of the resources of informatics helps us achieve more personal goals.

64. Preventing everything that harms children helps us achieve more successes.

65. Creative ideas help us achieve more favorable chances.

66. Persevering in ignoring the word NO helps us achieve more performances.

67. The passion of achieving personal goals helps us achieve much good luck.

68. The ability of not letting ourselves be stopped helps us achieve more favorable chances.

69. Setting high personal goals helps us achieve much good luck.

70. Our everyday effective actions help us achieve more efficient co operations.

71. Preventing everything that harms young people helps us achieve more successes.

72. The power of hope helps us achieve more true friendships.

73. The power used to accomplish positive deeds helps us achieve more favorable chances.

74. Preventing accidents helps us achieve more favorable situations.

75. Imposing respect helps us achieve more successes.

76. The desire to achieve performances helps us achieve more successes.

77. Positive ideas help us achieve more pleasant surprises.

78. The ability to go against everybody's convictions helps us achieve more successes.

79. Effective daily actions that are completed with passion help us achieve more favorable chances.

80. Never giving up helps us achieve more performances.

81. Will power helps us achieve more favorable chances.

82. The power of great dreams helps us achieve more favorable chances.

83. The faithfulness of collaborators helps us achieve more true friendships.

84. Knowing what is necessary for us to know helps us achieve more efficient co operations.

85. Keeping the focus on achieving personal goals helps us achieve more successes.

86. Preventing mistakes helps us achieve much good luck.

87. Our everyday effective actions help us achieve more successes.

88. Setting high personal goals helps us achieve more personal goals.

89. The art of solving misunderstandings helps us achieve more favorable situations.

90. Persevering in not letting ourselves be stopped helps us achieve more favorable situations.

91. Preventing accidents helps us achieve more performances.

92. Preventing inefficiencies helps us achieve more personal goals.

93. Learning how to solve problems helps us achieve more records.

94. The ability to solve misunderstandings helps us achieve more favorable chances.

95. Finding creative solutions to the problems helps us achieve more records.

96. Permanent concentration on our personal objectives helps us achieve more favorable situations.

97. The attitude of not letting ourselves be stopped helps us achieve more true friendships.

98. Knowing our profession helps us achieve more efficient co operations.

99. The strength of going against everybody's beliefs helps us achieve much good luck.

100. The willpower of not allowing ourselves to be stopped helps us achieve more efficient co operations.

101. The faithfulness of collaborators helps us achieve much good luck.

102. Passion for our work helps us achieve more true friendships.

103. Assuming initiatives helps us achieve more favorable situations.

104. Imitating positive deeds helps us achieve more true friendships.

105. Imposing respect helps us achieve more favorable chances.

106. The power of continuous efficient organization helps us achieve more performances.

107. Rising after a failure helps us achieve more efficient co operations.

108. The ability of achieving performances helps us achieve more favorable chances.

Accomplishments

109. We can contribute to the achievement of our greatest accomplishments also through the contribution of the formation, development, maintenance and usage of spiritual behavior.

110. We can contribute to the achievement of our greatest accomplishments also through the contribution of the formation, development, maintenance and usage of decent behavior.

111. We can contribute to the achievement of our greatest accomplishments also through the contribution of the formation, development, maintenance and usage of capable behavior.

112. We can contribute to the achievement of our greatest accomplishments also through the contribution of the formation, development, maintenance and usage of logical behavior.

113. We can contribute to the achievement of our greatest accomplishments also through the contribution of the formation, development, maintenance and usage of sincere behavior.

114. We can contribute to the achievement of our greatest accomplishments also through the contribution of the formation, development, maintenance and usage of voluble behavior.

115. We can contribute to the achievement of our greatest accomplishments also through the contribution of the formation, development, maintenance and usage of convincing behavior.

116. We can contribute to the achievement of our greatest accomplishments also through the contribution of the formation, development, maintenance and usage of tenacious behavior.

117. We can contribute to the achievement of our greatest accomplishments also through the contribution of the formation, development, maintenance and usage of positive behavior.

118. We can contribute to the achievement of our greatest accomplishments also through the contribution of the formation, development, maintenance and usage of self-controlled behavior.

119. We can contribute to the achievement of our greatest accomplishments also through the contribution of the formation, development, maintenance and usage of analytic behavior.

120. We can contribute to the achievement of our greatest accomplishments also through the contribution of the formation, development, maintenance and usage of prejudice-free behavior.

121. We can contribute to the achievement of our greatest accomplishments also through the contribution of the formation, development, maintenance and usage of attachable behavior.

122. We can contribute to the achievement of our greatest accomplishments also through the contribution of the formation, development, maintenance and usage of human behavior.

123. We can contribute to the achievement of our greatest accomplishments also through the contribution of the formation, development, maintenance and usage of spontaneous behavior.

124. We can contribute to the achievement of our greatest accomplishments also through the contribution of the formation, development,

maintenance and usage of independent behavior.

125. We can contribute to the achievement of our greatest accomplishments also through the contribution of the formation, development, maintenance and usage of cultivated behavior.

126. We can contribute to the achievement of our greatest accomplishments also through the contribution of the formation, development, maintenance and usage of strong behavior.

127. We can contribute to the achievement of our greatest accomplishments also through the contribution of the formation, development, maintenance and usage of productive behavior.

128. We can contribute to the achievement of our greatest accomplishments also through the contribution of the formation, development, maintenance and usage of continuous self-perfecting behavior.

129. We can contribute to the achievement of our greatest accomplishments also through the contribution of the formation, development, maintenance and usage of trained behavior.

130. We can contribute to the achievement of our greatest accomplishments also through the contribution of the formation, development,

maintenance and usage of demanding behavior.

131. We can contribute to the achievement of our greatest accomplishments also through the contribution of the formation, development, maintenance and usage of a behavior with theoretic spirit.

132. We can contribute to the achievement of our greatest accomplishments also through the contribution of the formation, development, maintenance and usage of optimistic behavior.

133. We can contribute to the achievement of our greatest accomplishments also through the contribution of the formation, development, maintenance and usage of perfectionist behavior.

Adaptable

134. Our happiness depends a lot also on the formation, development, maintenance and usage of adaptable behavior.

135. Some mistakes can be prevented also through the contribution of the formation, development, maintenance and usage of adaptable behavior.

136. Positive experience can be achieved also through the contribution of the formation,

development, maintenance and usage of adaptable behavior.

137. Wisdom helps us become adaptable.

138. The obstacles that prevent us from achieving our personal goals can be surpassed also through the contribution of the formation, development, maintenance and usage of adaptable behavior.

139. In order to prevent not achieving our personal goals, it is necessary to also form, develop, maintain and use our adaptable behavior.

140. Our resistance to changing for the better can be overcome also through the contribution of the formation, development, maintenance and usage of adaptable behavior.

141. Release from our self-imposed restrictions can be made also through the contribution of the formation, development, maintenance and usage of adaptable behavior.

142. We can become stronger and we can not allow ourselves to be influenced by the world also through the contribution of the formation, development, maintenance and usage of adaptable behavior.

143. We can form, develop and maintain the state of being ourselves also through the

contribution of the formation, development, maintenance and usage of an adaptable behavior.

144. Hopes can be created also through the contribution of the formation, development, maintenance and usage of adaptable behavior.

145. We can overcome the difficulties that we must overcome also through the help of the formation, development, maintenance and usage of adaptable behavior.

146. Optimism helps us become adaptable.

147. Cherishing oneself helps us become adaptable.

148. Rather than lamenting that we do not have successes it is more useful to also form, develop, maintain and use adaptable behavior.

149. Hope helps us become adaptable.

150. In achieving our successes a contribution is also brought by the formation, development, maintenance and usage of adaptable behavior.

151. Continuous self-motivation helps us become adaptable.

152. In order to escape poverty it is necessary to also form, develop, maintain and use adaptable behavior.

153. Stress can be prevented also through the formation, development, maintenance and usage of adaptable behavior.

154. Problems cannot be solved by the ideas that created them but also through the contribution of the formation, development, maintenance and usage of adaptable behavior.

155. We can prevent some failures also through the contribution of the formation, development, maintenance and usage of adaptable behavior.

156. The solutions to the problems we have or that we want to solve can be found also through the contribution of the formation, development, maintenance and usage of adaptable behavior.

157. The limits of achievement imposed by ourselves in our mind at a given moment can be overcome or eliminated also through the contribution of the formation, development, maintenance and usage of adaptable behavior.

158. Obtaining more and greater successes can be achieved also through the contribution of

the formation, development, maintenance, usage of an adaptable behavior.

Actions

159. Appreciating positive actions contributes to the achievement of other positive actions.

160. Life is a lot more pleasant when your positive actions are appreciated.

161. Appreciating positive actions makes those who do them stronger.

162. We must appreciate all of those who have positive actions.

163. We must always support those who have positive actions.

164. All positive actions contribute to the achievement of many other positive actions.

165. Positive actions must be rewarded.

166. Positive actions help us achieve more friendships.

167. Positive actions make our life a lot more beautiful.

168. Positive actions contribute to achieving personal goals.

169. All positive actions must be supported.

170. Positive actions must be supported.

171. Positive actions make us credible.

172. Positive human solidarity increases the efficiency of many human actions a lot.

173. Positive actions must be appreciated.

174. Positive actions prevent many negative surprises.

175. Positive actions must be imitated.

176. Constructive actions make us more credible.

177. Positive actions prevent many conflicts.

178. All positive actions must be rewarded.

179. In order to succeed it is necessary to form, develop, maintain and use the sense of efficiently planning our actions.

180. We can overcome difficulties also through the formation, development and support of the sense of positive actions.

181. The state of psychical discomfort can be removed through the formation, development and support of the ability to achieve efficient positive actions.

182. Our happiness depends a lot on the quality of our actions.

183. Discipline can be formed, developed and maintained by efficiently planning actions.

184. Obtaining as many and greatest successes as we can, can be achieved through the formation, development, maintenance and usage of the ability to achieve only efficient actions.

185. We can overcome difficulties through the formation, development and maintenance of efficient actions.

186. In order to pursue and transform positive objectives into reality it is necessary to form and develop a great ability to be efficient in positive actions.

187. In order to pursue and transform positive objectives into reality it is necessary to form, develop, maintain and use the ability to achieve efficient actions.

188. Our negative transformation can be avoided through the formation, development, maintenance and usage of efficient actions.

189. In order to change it is necessary to form, develop, maintain and use the ability to efficiently organize actions.

190. Positive experience can be achieved also through the contribution of the formation,

development and maintenance of the ability to efficiently organize our actions.

191. We can contribute to achieving our happiness also by efficiently organizing our actions.

192. In order to change our life it is necessary to form, develop, maintain and use the ability to achieve efficient actions.

193. Forming wrong ideas can be prevented also through the formation, development, maintenance and usage of the sense of efficiently planning positive actions.

194. In achieving successes a contribution is brought by the formation, development, maintenance and usage of the sense of efficiently planning actions.

195. Developing our thinking can be achieved and strengthened and we cannot read ourselves be influenced by the world also through the contribution of the formation, development, maintenance and usage of efficient actions.

196. In order to pursue and transform our personal goals into reality we need to form, develop, maintain and use the ability to efficiently organize our actions.

197. Obtaining as many and great successes that we can, can be achieved through the contribution of formation, development, maintenance and usage of a great ability to efficiently plan actions.

198. Our happiness depends a lot on the formation, development, maintenance and usage of the ability to be efficient in positive actions.

199. Successes are assured by legal actions.

200. Our transformation for the better can be achieved also through the contribution of the formation, development, maintenance and usage of the ability to plan our actions.

201. We can prevent some failures also through the contribution of the formation, development, maintenance and usage of the ability to achieve efficient actions.

202. In order to prevent failures it is necessary that we form, develop, maintain and use the sense of the efficient planning of actions.

203. Positive experience can be achieved also through the contribution of the formation, development, maintenance and usage of the ability to efficiently plan actions.

204. The state of psychical discomfort can be removed also through the formation,

development and maintenance of the sense of planning positive actions.

205. Emancipation from self imposed restrictions can be made through the formation, development and maintenance of planning our actions.

Activities

206. Presently, mankind wastes its resources for negative activities such as: producing cigarettes, producing arms that exceed the necessary of solving problems in a peaceful way, maintaining overpopulated armies, maintaining repressive forces used exaggeratedly, etc.

207. Good humor can be maintained through a balanced life, a proper diet, education, intellectual exercises, psychical balance, perseverance, women, physical exercises, a value system in which we believe in and that we respect, positive activities, dynamism, social relations, friends, mature love, a happy marriage, etc.

208. Only quality activities help us achieve effective co operations.

209. Only quality activities help us achieve successes.

210. Only activities as helping others take us towards achieving effective co operations.

211. Only activities as helping others take us towards achieving successes.

212. Positive human experience is very little recorded in writing, video and audio. It is necessary and imperative that the entire positive human experience be registered and used as much as possible in human activities.

213. The financing by the state of more positive, efficient initiatives, helpful to people and society should contribute a lot and would accelerate the development of their personality, their integration into society, from participating in the realization of many activities of society.

214. Although the activities of raising children are very important for a family and for society, unfortunately countries still allocate less money and fewer resources than they can.

215. The world does not provide the conditions necessary and mandatory for the activities necessary to achieve a performance in raising children and its importance.

216. People who are used to carrying out the activities they have started have the

capacity to achieve efficient co-developments.

217. People who are used to carrying out the activities they have started have greater chances to achieve personal goals.

218. An intelligent man is cooperative in activities.

219. Men cooperating in activities are more likely to maintain a happy marriage.

220. The young love and want to participate in social activities.

221. We can remove the feeling of loneliness through our involvement in positive activities as much as possible.

222. Involvement in positive activities is a necessity for all of us.

223. We can form the quality of social activities through the Internet by participating in debates in forums, in the creation of a forum, when we communicate with other people.

224. Single people can get rid of loneliness when involved in positive activities.

225. Involvement in positive activities helps us become more sociable.

226. Many who have bankrupted were also set up in a place where there were no commercial activities and then those who managed them did not know know to attract enough customers not to go bankrupt.

227. Each of us has had one or more bigger or smaller failures. It's good not to have any failures or as few failures as possible. Some or more failures could harm us very much. Those who were careful did not achieve failure or failures and have made smaller, fewer ones. Prevision helps us prevent many failures. The more experienced in previsioning we are, the greater ability we have to provide, as we have more knowledge necessary to achieve previsions etc.. the more we can make accurate previsions, prevent many mistakes, failures, trouble, accidents, conflicts, arguments, unsuccessful actions, etc. In our personal and professional life, it is necessary to continuously develop and to have that personal goal to develop to a maximum capacity the prevision in private life, the ability to use previsions. We can continuously increase the capacity of our prevision very much, as we live if we have personal objectives, as we expand our ability to prevision and whether we act to continuously and effectively achieve this objective. Those who aimed at personal

living as to develop the capacity of prevision continuously and concretely act with dedication to achieve their capacity to make a prevision which will help them achieve one or more very big successes, they will succeed to prevent many failures, troubles, etc., they will be able to achieve much in life, to have many happy, satisfying moments and so much happiness. The more we have a capacity of more than prevision, a more accurate, more efficient one, the more valuable we are for having this treasure. This treasure we can continuously increase greatly. The capacity of prevision generally contains more capacities of prevision in some actions, behaviors in the achievement of personal objectives, private, professional, specific ones, etc. It is necessary to develop those capabilities specific to prediction that we need. Knowledge, experience, qualifications, skills, etc., in a specific prevision capacity can be used to a greater or lesser degree in other capacities specific to prevision. The capacities of prevision are very necessary and very useful to us but unfortunately very few people have personal goals in life to continuously develop the specific performance of prevision. Due to the special importance of the capacity of prevision it is necessary and required to create and develop the science of the development of the capacity of prevision, because having this science we would have it by applying enormous positive effects on countless people that should develop and apply it indirectly on other people. The state would accelerate progress in many fields, would accelerate the reduction of illiteracy, poverty, illness, divorces out of arguments and conflict, accidents, what harms humans, animals, the environment, etc.. It would lead to solving many personal and state targets, it would create enormously many joys, much satisfaction and happiness. It would lead to the situation that most people no longer live at the whim of chance, with no personal, professional security, etc.. but on the contrary they would lead to more people having them as an objective and as they continue to live, they would develop the personal capacities necessary for their prevision and apply them every day, both in the establishment of private personal or professional life, it would be something concrete that will help them achieve more harmonious lives to achieve what they want and need for their families. There is the capacity of prevision in specific persons, specific societies, specific legal entities, nonprofit organizations, companies, banks, groups, collectivities, international and intergovernmental organizations. Both individuals and legal entities, must not live from hand to mouth, must act firmly, must study and evaluate the effects of positive and negative actions, decisions, etc. their objectives are also necessary to be: 1) to aim at continuing to develop their capacities of specific prediction that they need, 2) to apply, continuous use in any action, situation-specific prediction capabilities necessary and useful efforts, energy consumption and costs for the development and capacity of specific prevision that they need.

Failures can happen in each of our actions or less often. Our failures can be created by factors and actions sometimes difficult to identify and prevent. However there are actions where we can know all the factors that can create failures. Knowing the factors that create failures in actions, we can take the necessary measures to prevent them by reaching in some cases to zero failures, as they have succeeded in situations in a long time, in many states, especially people in the most developed countries of the world. How to develop more this science with the more than we can know more of the factors that could cause failures in certain situations to certain actions. Scientific knowledge can contribute greatly to preventing many failures in many actions. At present people do not use scientific knowledge, the human experience gained in books, studies, on the Internet, although they have committed enormously many failures, mistakes, although they could prevent many huge mistakes, failures if they would use efficient, organized, timely human experience and knowledge from books, the Internet when they would need it. Countries should take immediate measures and be more interested in people and use them when they need knowledge and human experience that can reach and can be used. Human knowledge is growing and increases daily awfully much, and human experience which can create the situation so that we can prevent every day more even more mistakes and failures with positive effects on our high society, to accelerate progress in many areas. Where we have failures we should never discourage and lose our wits, our balance inside, our optimism, morale or to start to grieve. If we do this, it would solve absolutely no problem, but on the contrary, it would stress us illogically, abnormally without any positive effects. Those who have achieved many successes knew how to cope with failure, learning from failures, to reduce the negative effects of failures. Many failures rather than strengthening us, they weaken us, they should give us power instead of imobilizing us and mobilize us instead of making them harder to give motivation, instead of multiple negative effects they should have have multiple positive effects.

However, I disagree and do not consider as logical, positive or constructive the popular saying: „Man learns from mistakes". Man, on the contrary should learn only from his successes and from those who have achieved successes and gained, by imitating those positive behaviors, which have effectively contributed to success. In addition man can learn enormously not to have failures, or make mistakes from the knowledge and positive experience of mankind stored in books, media, on the Internet and the experience of people who have huge experience and knowledge. The more we can prevent more failures, mistakes, the more we can prevent more and more different negative effects. It would be necessary and useful the development of a science to prevent human errors because it would prevent a large number of human errors and failures if people study and apply it as much and in as many actions as they can. This knowledge could and should be studied in colleges and universities and other educational forms. In every area of activity for each action type, it could identify factors that create human mistakes and failures and then it could identify solutions and measures to be taken to prevent mistakes and failures.

Efforts and expenses that will be done by creating, developing, learning and applicating the science to prevent human errors will not be much lower than the positive effects of their prevention of a very large number of mistakes and failures and their multiple, diverse and very large negative effects. Financial investment, energy, time, etc.. in these activities related to the prevention of human errors and failures would be very effective and necessary and useful for both countries and for people in particular. Each of us in a greater or lesser way can participate in the creation, development and application of the science to prevent human errors.

228. Persons with success, models of their effective actions give us a positive incentive to achieve our objectives and personal milestones. For this reason, and that we can take positive and effective behavior from them, it is necessary to take more of their positive activities to effectively increase our efficiency and more our actions and achieve our personal goals.

229. True friends can help us enormously to achieve our happiness and we, in turn, help them achieve theirs. We can much easier make both new and true friends as our objectives to help us become happy. This

makes us have a special care and concern, with much dedication to form, develop and maintain relations of true friends and mutual activities, common actions, etc..

230. It is much more effective, humane, legal, responsible, necessary and required for society to prevent the causes leading to situations in which some people have the need for human protection and to ensure the human protection of people who need it rather than: 1) build prisons, 2) increase the number of police, gendarmerie and other repressive forces. 3) spend large sums on various formal activities of the state's institutions without any actual positive finality, etc.

231. Thinking long term refers to long term projects, actions, activities.

232. Short-term thinking refers to short term projects, actions, activities, etc.

233. We can encounter more easily favorable situations for us if we continue to focus on our activities.

234. The transparency of the institutions' activities prevents many acts of corruption.

235. Spiritual self-development helps and contributes greatly to self-progress in other actions and activities.

236. Although many scientific researches have found that smoking damages very much our health, even that of those who are non-smokers, all countries accept the legal industry and related trade of cigarettes, which cause tens and hundreds of millions of illnesses and deaths. The situation is incredible, but unfortunately, it exists in all of the world's states. Why do we even tolerate such incredibly damageable activities for billions of people, with incalculable negative effects?

Anticipating

237. A great capacity of anticipating helps us become more cautious.

238. A great capacity of anticipating helps us achieve more personal goals.

239. A great capacity of anticipating helps us become humane.

240. A great capacity of anticipating helps us maintain our way of being cautious.

241. A great capacity of anticipating helps us become more humane.

242. A great capacity of anticipating helps us become loving.

243. A great capacity of anticipating helps us maintain our way of being understanding.

244. A great capacity of anticipating helps us maintain our tolerance.

245. A great capacity of anticipating must be used.

246. A great capacity of anticipating helps us maintain our efficiency.

247. A great capacity of anticipating helps us maintain our way of being practical.

248. A great capacity of anticipating helps us achieve more favorable situations.

249. A great capacity of anticipating helps us become enthusiastic.

250. A great capacity of anticipating helps us become productive.

251. A great capacity of anticipating helps us maintain our enthusiasm.

252. A great capacity of anticipating helps us become wise.

253. We can form, develop, maintain and use an open mind also through contribution of the formation, development, maintenance and usage of anticipating behavior.

254. The capacity of anticipating people's needs helps us a lot to make those people happy.

255. The capacity of anticipating people's needs helps us achieve more efficient co operations.

256. The capacity of anticipating people's needs helps us maintain our efficient co-developments.

257. The ability of anticipating people's needs helps us more easily achieve our personal goals.

258. The ability of anticipating people's needs helps us achieve more and greater successes.

259. The ability of anticipating people's needs helps us understand them a lot better.

Analytic

260. Our resistance to changing for the better can be overcome also through the contribution of the formation, development, maintenance and usage of analytic behavior.

261. Pessimism can be removed and replaced with optimism also through the contribution of the formation, development, maintenance and usage of analytic behavior.

262. Continuously making ourselves efficient helps us become analytic.

263. Positive experience can be achieved also through the contribution of the formation, development, maintenance and usage of analytic behavior.

264. Continuous self perfection helps us become analytic.

265. Self-imposed discipline helps us become analytic.

266. Wisdom helps us become analytic.

267. Our future can be projected and achieved also through the contribution of the formation, development, maintenance and usage of analytic behavior.

268. Obtaining more and greater successes can be achieved also through the contribution of the formation, development, maintenance, usage of analytical thinking.

269. Acting efficiently helps us become analytic.

270. The limits of achievement imposed by ourselves in our mind at a given moment can be overcome or eliminated also through the contribution of the formation, development, maintenance and usage of analytic behavior.

271. Continuous self-motivation helps us become analytic.

272. Rather than lamenting that we do not have successes it is more useful to also form, develop, maintain and use analytic behavior.

273. Will helps us become analytic.

274. The obstacles that prevent us from achieving our personal goals can be surpassed also through the contribution of the formation, development, maintenance and usage of analytic behavior.

275. Hopes can be created also through the contribution of the formation, development, maintenance and usage of analytic behavior.

276. Obtaining more and greater successes can be achieved also through the contribution of the formation, development, maintenance, usage of an analytic behavior.

277. In order to escape poverty it is necessary to also form, develop, maintain and use analytic behavior.

278. Continuous self-motivation helps us become analytical.

279. Aspiring towards a more meaningful life can also be achieved through the formation,

development, maintenance and usage of analytic behavior.

280. Creativity helps us become analytic.

281. Stress can be prevented also through the formation, development, maintenance and usage of analytic behavior.

282. Problems cannot be solved by the ideas that created them but also through the contribution of the formation, development, maintenance and usage of analytic behavior.

283. Confidence in ourselves helps us become analytic.

284. In order to follow and transform our personal goals into reality, it is necessary to also form, develop, maintain and use our analytic behavior.

Attitudes

285. A great capacity of using attitudes must be rewarded.

286. A great capacity of using attitudes helps us achieve more true friendships.

287. A great capacity of using attitudes helps us maintain our way of being loved.

288. A great capacity of using attitudes helps us become more tolerant.

289. A great capacity of using attitudes helps us become enthusiastic.

290. A great capacity of using attitudes must be used.

291. A great capacity of using attitudes helps us become more practical.

292. A great capacity of using attitudes helps us maintain our way of being liked.

293. A great capacity of using attitudes helps us achieve more records.

294. A great capacity of using attitudes helps us become more loved.

295. A great capacity of using attitudes helps us become more cautious.

296. A great capacity of using attitudes helps us become humane.

297. A great capacity of using attitudes helps us become more pleasant.

298. A great capacity of using attitudes must be appreciated.

299. A great capacity of using attitudes helps us achieve more performances.

300. A great capacity of using attitudes helps us achieve more pleasant surprises.

301. A great capacity of using attitudes helps us achieve more efficient co operations.

302. A great capacity of using attitudes helps us maintain our way of being cautious.

303. A great capacity of using attitudes helps us maintain our way of being practical.

304. A great capacity of using attitudes helps us become cautious.

305. A great capacity of using attitudes helps us become practical.

306. A great capacity of using attitudes helps us maintain our way of being loving.

307. A great capacity of using attitudes must be developed.

308. A great capacity of using attitudes helps us become more understanding.

309. A great capacity of using attitudes helps us become happy.

Become

310. A great capacity of self-surpassing helps us become more humane.

311. A great capacity of succeeding in every way helps us become optimistic.

312. The self efficient use of our time helps us become peaceful.

313. A great capacity of persevering until finding creative solutions helps us become loving.

314. A great capacity of thinking largely helps us become more preventive.

315. A great capacity of teaching people helps us become more understanding.

316. Hope helps us become independent.

317. Self-imposed discipline helps us become audacious.

318. Self-imposed discipline helps us become confident.

319. Continuously making ourselves efficient helps us become vivacious.

320. A great capacity of working hard helps us become loved.

321. Optimism helps us become voluble.

322. A great capacity of being brave helps us become more efficient.

323. Continuous self perfection helps us become firm.

324. A great capacity of assuming the necessary risks for achieving great successes helps us become more practical.

325. A great capacity of forming a positive own lifestyle helps us become more loved.

326. Continuous self-motivation helps us become pleasant.

327. A great capacity of assuming the necessary risks for success helps us become more pleasant.

328. A great capacity of being flexible helps us become more cautious.

329. A great capacity of enjoying work helps us become more understanding.

330. A great capacity of maintaining relationships with people helps us become more enthusiastic.

331. A great capacity of continuously enhancing performances helps us become more enthusiastic.

332. Wisdom helps us become perfectionists.

333. A great capacity of being convincing helps us become more enthusiastic.

334. Acting efficiently helps us become eager for knowledge.

335. Acting efficiently helps us become spiritual.

336. We can become stronger and we can not allow ourselves to be influenced by the world also through the contribution of the formation, development, maintenance and usage of astute behavior.

337. Acting efficiently helps us become tenacious.

338. Wisdom helps us become profound.

339. A great capacity of continuous self perfection helps us become enthusiastic.

340. Wisdom helps us become active.

341. A great capacity of using each personal mistake to achieve successes helps us become productive.

342. A great capacity of continuously overcoming boundaries helps us become enthusiastic.

343. The desire to be grand helps us become more productive.

344. A great capacity of not letting others lead one's life helps us become tolerant.

345. A great capacity of assuming the necessary risks for success helps us become productive.

346. A great capacity of assuming the necessary risks for success helps us become more efficient.

347. A great capacity of continuously overcoming boundaries helps us become more loved.

348. A great capacity of anticipating helps us become happy.

349. Confidence in ourselves helps us become loved.

350. A great capacity of establishing even greater personal goals helps us become more efficient.

351. A great capacity of having an even more energetic life helps us become more efficient.

352. A great capacity of maintaining relationships with people helps us become optimistic.

353. A great capacity of drawing attention helps us become optimistic.

354. A great capacity of using each injustice received in order to achieve successes helps us become practical.

355. A great capacity of being friendly helps us become more preventive.

356. A great capacity of assuming the necessary risks for achieving great successes helps us become more tolerant.

357. Responsibility helps us become peacemakers.

358. A great capacity of persevering until finding creative solutions helps us become productive.

359. A great capacity of having an even more energetic life helps us become happier.

360. Acting efficiently helps us become complex.

361. We can become stronger and we can not allow ourselves to be influenced by the world also through the contribution of the formation, development, maintenance and usage of daring behavior.

362. The dream to the grand helps us become tolerant.

363. A great capacity of being popular helps us become more optimistic.

364. A great capacity of positively influencing people helps us become more loved.

365. A great capacity of maintaining relationships with people helps us become more pleasant.

366. A great capacity of continuously enhancing performances helps us become more productive.

367. Continuously making ourselves efficient helps us become leaders.

368. Continuous self-control helps us become cheerful.

369. A great capacity of using available resources helps us become more humane.

370. A great capacity of thinking largely helps us become happier.

371. A great capacity of encouraging people helps us become more humane.

372. A great capacity of establishing high personal goals helps us become more productive.

373. A great capacity of using available knowledge helps us become happier.

374. Continuous self-motivation helps us become devoid of prejudices.

375. Responsibility helps us become loyal.

376. Acting efficiently helps us become expansive.

377. Acting efficiently helps us become hard-working.

378. Optimism helps us become kind.

379. The self efficient use of our time helps us become idealistic.

380. Will helps us become kind.

381. Continuously making ourselves efficient helps us become wise.

382. Communication helps us become diplomatic.

383. A great capacity of assuming the necessary risks for success helps us become more optimistic.

384. Acting efficiently helps us become with scientific spirit.

385. Optimism helps us become good listeners.

386. A great capacity of being honest with oneself helps us become more humane.

387. Continuous self-motivation helps us become tenacious.

388. A great capacity of using each failure to achieve successes helps us become happy.

389. A great capacity of appreciating people helps us become more tolerant.

390. Communication helps us become energetic.

391. A great capacity of being friendly helps us become optimistic.

392. A great capacity of not letting others lead one's life helps us become more optimistic.

393. Acting efficiently helps us become analytical.

394. A great capacity of succeeding in every way helps us become practical.

395. A great capacity of being wise helps us become tolerant.

396. Communication helps us become daring.

397. A great capacity of positively influencing people helps us become more loving.

398. Self-imposed discipline helps us become trustworthy.

399. A great capacity of using available resources helps us become enthusiastic.

400. A great capacity of gathering our energies helps us become more humane.

401. A great capacity of being friendly helps us become more enthusiastic.

402. Optimism helps us become meticulous.

403. A great capacity of being understanding with people helps us become more tolerant.

404. A great capacity of investing efficiently helps us become efficient.

405. Creativity helps us become firm.

406. The self efficient use of our time helps us become consequent.

407. Continuous self perfection helps us become fighting.

408. A great capacity of thinking largely helps us become more productive.

409. Hope helps us become flexible.

410. A great capacity of being understanding with people helps us become more preventive.

411. A great capacity of encouraging people helps us become happier.

412. Will helps us become daring.

413. The dream to the grand helps us become loving.

414. A great capacity of being creative in order to solve great problems helps us become loved.

415. A great capacity of doing what is best helps us become more loving.

416. Will helps us become penetrating.

417. A great capacity of more efficiently using financial means helps us become more understanding.

418. A great capacity of forming a positive own lifestyle helps us become more cautious.

419. Perseverance helps us become preventive.

420. A great capacity of being flexible helps us become optimistic.

421. A great capacity of learning how to achieve personal goals helps us become productive.

422. A great capacity of gathering our energies helps us become more tolerant.

423. A great capacity of cherishing oneself helps us become more loved.

424. A great capacity of having an even more energetic life helps us become more preventive.

425. A great capacity of adopting visions helps us become more cautious.

426. A great capacity of accomplishing strategies of applying thinking on a big scale helps us become more efficient.

427. Acting efficiently helps us become docile.

428. The desire to be grand helps us become loved.

429. A great capacity of thinking largely helps us become wise.

430. A great capacity of using abilities helps us become more optimistic.

431. Will helps us become decisive.

432. A great capacity of continuously overcoming boundaries helps us become more cautious.

433. Continuous self-control helps us become organized.

434. Hope helps us become trained.

Behavior

435. Rather than lamenting that we do not have successes it is more useful to also form, develop, maintain and use selfless behavior.

436. Problems cannot be solved by the ideas that created them but also through the contribution of the formation, development, maintenance and usage of joyful behavior.

437. Positive experience can be achieved also through the contribution of the formation, development, maintenance and usage of adaptable behavior.

438. We can prevent some failures also through the contribution of the formation, development, maintenance and usage of animated behavior.

439. Obtaining more and greater successes can be achieved also through the contribution of the formation, development, maintenance, usage of a cheerful behavior.

440. Our future can be projected and achieved also through the contribution of the formation, development, maintenance and usage of a behavior of being inclined towards research.

441. We can contribute to the achievement of our greatest accomplishments also through the contribution of the formation, development, maintenance and usage of joyful behavior.

442. Some mistakes can be prevented also through the contribution of the formation,

development, maintenance and usage of capable behavior.

443. The force of our ideas can be augmented also through the contribution of the formation, development, maintenance and usage of optimistic behavior.

444. Rather than lamenting that we do not have successes it is more useful to also form, develop, maintain and use imaginative behavior.

445. The obstacles that prevent us from achieving our personal goals can be surpassed also through the contribution of the formation, development, maintenance and usage of unpretentious behavior.

446. Pessimism can be removed and replaced with optimism also through the contribution of the formation, development, maintenance and usage of brave behavior.

447. The necessary qualities in achieving personal goals can be formed, developed, maintained and used also through the contribution of the formation, development, maintenance and usage of continuous self economizing behavior.

448. In order to prevent failures it is necessary to also form, develop, maintain and use trained behavior.

449. Pessimism can be removed and replaced with optimism also through the contribution of the formation, development, maintenance and usage of demanding behavior.

450. Stress can be prevented also through the formation, development, maintenance and usage of profound behavior.

451. We can prevent some failures also through the contribution of the formation, development, maintenance and usage of stimulating behavior.

452. The limits of achievement imposed by ourselves in our mind at a given moment can be overcome or eliminated also through the contribution of the formation, development, maintenance and usage of a behavior with a scientific spirit.

453. The necessary qualities in achieving personal goals can be formed, developed, maintained and used also through the contribution of the formation, development, maintenance and usage of kind behavior.

454. Our happiness depends a lot also on the formation, development, maintenance and usage of a behavior of being eager for knowledge.

455. The limits of achievement imposed by ourselves in our mind at a given moment

can be overcome or eliminated also through the contribution of the formation, development, maintenance and usage of continuous self-motivating behavior.

456. Our resistance to changing for the better can be overcome also through the contribution of the formation, development, maintenance and usage of sturdy behavior.

457. Obtaining more and greater successes can be achieved also through the contribution of the formation, development, maintenance, usage of a peacemaking behavior.

458. In order to rise up once again for the first time for the who knows what time it is necessary to also form, develop, maintain and use harmless behavior.

459. Stress can be prevented also through the formation, development, maintenance and usage of leading behavior.

460. Our future can be projected and achieved also through the contribution of the formation, development, maintenance and usage of spiritual behavior.

461. Aspiring towards a more meaningful life can also be achieved through the formation, development, maintenance and usage of a behavior of being devoid of prejudices.

462. Some mistakes can be prevented also through the contribution of the formation, development, maintenance and usage of a behavior with a scientific spirit.

463. Pessimism can be removed and replaced with optimism also through the contribution of the formation, development, maintenance and usage of sociable behavior.

464. We can overcome the difficulties that we must overcome also through the help of the formation, development, maintenance and usage of a behavior of being eager for knowledge.

465. Our resistance to changing for the better can be overcome also through the contribution of the formation, development, maintenance and usage of trained behavior.

466. In achieving our successes a contribution is also brought by the formation, development, maintenance and usage of loyal behavior.

467. Our future can be projected and achieved also through the contribution of the formation, development, maintenance and usage of sociable behavior.

468. The limits of achievement imposed by ourselves in our mind at a given moment can be overcome or eliminated also through the contribution of the formation,

development, maintenance and usage of continuous self-educating behavior.

469. In order to prevent failures it is necessary to also form, develop, maintain and use a behavior devoid of prejudices.

470. We can prevent the falling apart of a happy marriage also through the contribution of the formation, development, maintenance and usage of popular behavior.

471. Some mistakes can be prevented also through the contribution of the formation, development, maintenance and usage of attachable behavior.

472. Positive experience can be achieved also through the contribution of the formation, development, maintenance and usage of meticulous behavior.

473. Pessimism can be removed and replaced with optimism also through the contribution of the formation, development, maintenance and usage of impersonal behavior.

474. We can overcome the difficulties that we must overcome also through the help of the formation, development, maintenance and usage of persevering behavior.

475. Pessimism can be removed and replaced with optimism also through the contribution

of the formation, development, maintenance and usage of scientific spirit behavior.

476. In achieving our successes a contribution is also brought by the formation, development, maintenance and usage of respectful behavior.

477. Problems cannot be solved by the ideas that created them but also through the contribution of the formation, development, maintenance and usage of funny behavior.

478. In order to rise up once again for the first time for the who knows what time it is necessary to also form, develop, maintain and use attachable behavior.

479. Positive experience can be achieved also through the contribution of the formation, development, maintenance and usage of a behavior of being in love with life.

480. Our own happiness can be achieved and maintained also through the contribution of the formation, development, maintenance and usage of fighting behavior.

481. We can prevent some failures also through the contribution of the formation, development, maintenance and usage of reserved behavior.

482. We can become stronger and we can not allow ourselves to be influenced by the world also through the contribution of the formation, development, maintenance and usage of astute behavior.

483. Problems cannot be solved by the ideas that created them but also through the contribution of the formation, development, maintenance and usage of a behavior of being eager for knowledge.

484. We can overcome the difficulties that we must overcome also through the help of the formation, development, maintenance and usage of voluble behavior.

485. Rather than lamenting that we do not have successes it is more useful to also form, develop, maintain and use animated behavior.

486. Some mistakes can be prevented also through the contribution of the formation, development, maintenance and usage of vivacious behavior.

487. Aspiring towards a more meaningful life can also be achieved through the formation, development, maintenance and usage of continuous self motivating behavior.

488. We can contribute to the achievement of our greatest accomplishments also through the

contribution of the formation, development, maintenance and usage of continuous self-control behavior.

489. In order to prevent failures it is necessary to also form, develop, maintain and use reasonable behavior.

490. The radical transformation for the better of our life can be achieved also through the formation, development, maintenance and usage of reserved behavior.

491. Some mistakes can be prevented also through the contribution of the formation, development, maintenance and usage of docile behavior.

492. We can contribute to the achievement of our greatest accomplishments also through the contribution of the formation, development, maintenance and usage of inventive behavior.

493. Our own happiness can be achieved and maintained also through the contribution of the formation, development, maintenance and usage of sportive behavior.

494. The force of our ideas can be augmented also through the contribution of the formation, development, maintenance and usage of demanding behavior.

495. Our future can be projected and achieved also through the contribution of the formation, development, maintenance and usage of loyal behavior.

496. The necessary qualities in achieving personal goals can be formed, developed, maintained and used also through the contribution of the formation, development, maintenance and usage of charming behavior.

497. In achieving our successes a contribution is also brought by the formation, development, maintenance and usage of scientific spirit behavior.

498. Our future can be projected and achieved also through the contribution of the formation, development, maintenance and usage of inventive behavior.

499. Rather than lamenting that we do not have successes it is more useful to also form, develop, maintain and use of continuously self perfecting behavior.

500. Obtaining more and greater successes can be achieved also through the contribution of the formation, development, maintenance, usage of a responsible behavior.

501. Release from our self-imposed restrictions can be made also through the contribution of

the formation, development, maintenance and usage of a behavior with a scientific spirit.

502. The obstacles that prevent us from achieving our personal goals can be surpassed also through the contribution of the formation, development, maintenance and usage of continuous self-controlling behavior.

503. Obtaining more and greater successes can be achieved also through the contribution of the formation, development, maintenance, usage of a patient behavior.

504. Our resistance to changing for the better can be overcome also through the contribution of the formation, development, maintenance and usage of realistic behavior.

505. The necessary qualities in achieving personal goals can be formed, developed, maintained and used also through the contribution of the formation, development, maintenance and usage of peaceful behavior.

506. Obtaining more and greater successes can be achieved also through the contribution of the formation, development, maintenance, usage of an organized behavior.

507. The solutions to the problems we have or that we want to solve can be found also through the contribution of the formation, development, maintenance and usage of animated behavior.

508. We can prevent the falling apart of a happy marriage also through the contribution of the formation, development, maintenance and usage of docile behavior.

509. We can become stronger and we can not allow ourselves to be influenced by the world also through the contribution of the formation, development, maintenance and usage of daring behavior.

510. Aspiring towards a more meaningful life can also be achieved through the formation, development, maintenance and usage of ingenious behavior.

511. The necessary qualities in achieving personal goals can be formed, developed, maintained and used also through the contribution of the formation, development, maintenance and usage of spiritual behavior.

512. The obstacles that prevent us from achieving our personal goals can be surpassed also through the contribution of

the formation, development, maintenance and usage of loyal behavior.

513. Problems cannot be solved by the ideas that created them but also through the contribution of the formation, development, maintenance and usage of brave behavior.

514. Our future can be projected and achieved also through the contribution of the formation, development, maintenance and usage of animated behavior.

515. The radical transformation for the better of our life can be achieved also through the formation, development, maintenance and usage of persevering behavior.

516. Obtaining more and greater successes can be achieved also through the contribution of the formation, development, maintenance, usage of a realistic behavior.

517. In order to prevent failures it is necessary to also form, develop, maintain and use spontaneous behavior.

518. The radical transformation for the better of our life can be achieved also through the formation, development, maintenance and usage of charitable behavior.

519. In achieving our successes a contribution is also brought by the formation, development,

maintenance and usage of sportive behavior.

520. Pessimism can be removed and replaced with optimism also through the contribution of the formation, development, maintenance and usage of calm behavior.

521. In order to prevent failures it is necessary to also form, develop, maintain and use convincing behavior.

522. The obstacles that prevent us from achieving our personal goals can be surpassed also through the contribution of the formation, development, maintenance and usage of ingenious behavior.

523. We can prevent some failures also through the contribution of the formation, development, maintenance and usage of receptive to new behavior.

524. Obtaining more and greater successes can be achieved also through the contribution of the formation, development, maintenance, usage of an expansive behavior.

525. The force of our ideas can be augmented also through the contribution of the formation, development, maintenance and usage of reasonable behavior.

526. Our future can be projected and achieved also through the contribution of the formation, development, maintenance and usage of cautious behavior.

527. The radical transformation for the better of our life can be achieved also through the formation, development, maintenance and usage of astute behavior.

528. Rather than lamenting that we do not have successes it is more useful to also form, develop, maintain and use tenacious behavior.

529. Our happiness depends a lot also on the formation, development, maintenance and usage of confident behavior.

530. We can prevent some failures also through the contribution of the formation, development, maintenance and usage of astute behavior.

531. In order to rise up once again for the first time for the who knows what time it is necessary to also form, develop, maintain and use decent behavior.

532. Release from our self-imposed restrictions can be made also through the contribution of the formation, development, maintenance and usage of reasonable behavior.

533. Obtaining more and greater successes can be achieved also through the contribution of the formation, development, maintenance, usage of a good listener behavior.

534. We can prevent some failures also through the contribution of the formation, development, maintenance and usage of continuous self perfecting behavior.

535. Pessimism can be removed and replaced with optimism also through the contribution of the formation, development, maintenance and usage of agreeable behavior.

536. We can prevent the falling apart of a happy marriage also through the contribution of the formation, development, maintenance and usage of pleasant behavior.

537. In order to prevent failures it is necessary to also form, develop, maintain and use impersonal behavior.

538. Release from our self-imposed restrictions can be made also through the contribution of the formation, development, maintenance and usage of optimistic behavior.

539. The radical transformation for the better of our life can be achieved also through the formation, development, maintenance and usage of efficient behavior.

540. The force of our ideas can be augmented also through the contribution of the formation, development, maintenance and usage of sensitive behavior.

541. Hopes can be created also through the contribution of the formation, development, maintenance and usage of constant behavior.

542. Our own happiness can be achieved and maintained also through the contribution of the formation, development, maintenance and usage of ordered behavior.

543. Some mistakes can be prevented also through the contribution of the formation, development, maintenance and usage of continuous self-motivating behavior.

544. Aspiring towards a more meaningful life can also be achieved through the formation, development, maintenance and usage of continuous control of the self behavior.

545. Pessimism can be removed and replaced with optimism also through the contribution of the formation, development, maintenance and usage of sincere behavior.

546. Stress can be prevented also through the formation, development, maintenance and usage of persevering behavior.

547. The force of our ideas can be augmented also through the contribution of the formation, development, maintenance and usage of intellectual behavior.

548. Our resistance to changing for the better can be overcome also through the contribution of the formation, development, maintenance and usage of a behavior with a scientific spirit.

549. Our own happiness can be achieved and maintained also through the contribution of the formation, development, maintenance and usage of voluble behavior.

550. Our own happiness can be achieved and maintained also through the contribution of the formation, development, maintenance and usage of diplomatic behavior.

551. The solutions to the problems we have or that we want to solve can be found also through the contribution of the formation, development, maintenance and usage of enthusiastic behavior.

552. The force of our ideas can be augmented also through the contribution of the formation, development, maintenance and usage of the loyal behavior.

553. In order to escape poverty it is necessary to also form, develop, maintain and use joyful behavior.

554. Our resistance to changing for the better can be overcome also through the contribution of the formation, development, maintenance and usage of stimulating behavior.

555. The limits of achievement imposed by ourselves in our mind at a given moment can be overcome or eliminated also through the contribution of the formation, development, maintenance and usage of tenacious behavior.

556. Some mistakes can be prevented also through the contribution of the formation, development, maintenance and usage of realistic behavior.

557. The necessary qualities in achieving personal goals can be formed, developed, maintained and used also through the contribution of the formation, development, maintenance and usage of humane behavior.

558. Hopes can be created also through the contribution of the formation, development, maintenance and usage of spontaneous behavior.

559. Release from our self-imposed restrictions can be made also through the contribution of the formation, development, maintenance and usage of peaceful behavior.

Bold

560. We can prevent the falling apart of a happy marriage also through the contribution of the formation, development, maintenance and usage of bold behavior.

561. Problems cannot be solved by the ideas that created them but also through the contribution of the formation, development, maintenance and usage of bold behavior.

562. The self efficient use of our time helps us become bold.

563. In order to prevent failures it is necessary to also form, develop, maintain and use bold behavior.

564. Wisdom helps us become bold.

565. The solutions to the problems we have or that we want to solve can be found also through the contribution of the formation,

development, maintenance and usage of bold behavior.

566. Continuous self-motivation helps us become bold.

567. Continuous self perfection helps us become bold.

568. Continuously making ourselves efficient helps us become bold.

569. Will helps us become bold.

570. Obtaining more and greater successes can be achieved also through the contribution of the formation, development, maintenance, usage of a bold behavior.

571. Hopes can be created also through the contribution of the formation, development, maintenance and usage of bold behavior.

572. We can become stronger and we can not allow ourselves to be influenced by the world also through the contribution of the formation, development, maintenance and usage of bold behavior.

573. Our resistance to changing for the better can be overcome also through the contribution of the formation, development, maintenance and usage of bold behavior.

574. Responsibility helps us become bold.

575. Our happiness depends a lot also on the formation, development, maintenance and usage of bold behavior.

576. Hope helps us become bold.

577. We can contribute to the achievement of our greatest accomplishments also through the contribution of the formation, development, maintenance and usage of bold behavior.

578. The limits of achievement imposed by ourselves in our mind at a given moment can be overcome or eliminated also through the contribution of the formation, development, maintenance and usage of bold behavior.

579. Pessimism can be removed and replaced with optimism also through the contribution of the formation, development, maintenance and usage of bold behavior.

580. Optimism helps us become bold.

581. Self-imposed discipline helps us become bold.

582. The force of our ideas can be augmented also through the contribution of the formation, development, maintenance and usage of bold behavior.

583. Rather than lamenting that we do not have successes it is more useful to also form, develop, maintain and use bold behavior.

584. Acting efficiently helps us become bold.

585. Confidence in ourselves helps us become bold.

586. The obstacles that prevent us from achieving our personal goals can be surpassed also through the contribution of the formation, development, maintenance and usage of bold behavior.

587. In order to escape poverty it is necessary to also form, develop, maintain and use bold behavior.

588. Our own happiness can be achieved and maintained also through the contribution of the formation, development, maintenance and usage of bold behavior.

589. Some mistakes can be prevented also through the contribution of the formation, development, maintenance and usage of bold behavior.

590. In order to prevent not achieving our personal goals, it is necessary to also form, develop, maintain and use our bold behavior.

591. Good sense is not that of a bold man.

592. Those who have no sense are often also bold.

Capacities

593. It is always needed to develop capacities, skills, qualities and attitudes, but we need the development of our personality, it is necessary to have this as a personal objective.

594. I am not saying that women should not be concerned with their outer beauty but to occupy themselves more with their inner beauty, to achieve and maintain a happy marriage. For these targets women fortunately have unlimited capacities but unfortunately very few use them.

595. Young people from many countries of the world by filling seats that they can in local councils, central ones, in the parliament, government and other institutions and by maximizing the use of the resources available (energy, enthusiasm, optimism, devotion, capacities, values, skills, abilities, knowledge, etc.) can contribute enormously much to accelerating the solving of many

problems of their regims, of their goals, and of the world.

596. Young people from all of the world's states should not be negligent, careless, passive, inactive, non-participative in taking decisions that concern them, their present and future, but to take part in decision-making in local councils, central parliaments, governments and other state and non-state institutions, and use all their capacities, abilities, skills, attitudes, knowledge, energy, commitment and desire to assert and achieve great deeds, to create a more humane, more righteous, more happy, with less trouble world.

597. Young people of the world's states, unfortunately, do not use their capacities and qualities, skills, abilities, attitudes, knowledge, and the enormous energy that they have, their enthusiasm and optimism, which are positive things, the desire of affirmation and of making achievements in order to participate in the activity of communal, municipal, departmental, regional councils of counties, of parliaments, of governments, etc..

Calm

598. In order to prevent failures it is necessary to also form, develop, maintain and use calm behavior.

599. Calm people prevent more trouble in all situations.

600. People who are calm in any situation prevent many conflicts.

601. People who are calm in almost all situations prevent a lot of unpleasant surprises.

602. People who are calm in all situations make fewer mistakes.

603. People who are calm in any situation are more credible.

604. Our own personality can be maintained through the ability to be calm in any stressing situation.

605. We can achieve our personal goals also through the formation, development, maintenance and usage of the ability to be calm in any situation.

606. Obtaining as many and greatest successes as we can, can be achieved through the formation, development and maintenance of the ability to be calm in any situation.

607. Emancipation from restrictions can be made through the formation, development and maintenance of the ability to be calm in any situation.

608. In order to pursue and transform our personal goals into reality we need to form, develop, maintain and use the ability to be calm in stressing situations.

609. Positive experience can be achieved also through the contribution of the formation, development and maintenance of the ability to be calm in stressing situations.

610. Preventing stress can be achieved also through the contribution of the formation, development, maintenance and usage of calm behaviors.

611. In order to pursue and transform our personal goals into reality we need to form and develop the ability to be calm in stressing situations.

612. We can prevent some failures also through the contribution of the formation, development, maintenance and usage of calm behaviors.

613. Aspiring towards a more meaningful life can be achieved also through the contribution of the formation, development, maintenance

and usage of the ability to be calm in any stressing situation.

614. In order to pursue and transform our personal goals into reality we need to form, develop, maintain and use the ability to be calm in any stressing situation.

615. A radical transformation for the better of our life can be achieved also through the contribution of the formation, development, maintenance and usage of the ability to be calm in any stressing situation.

616. In order to trace and transform our personal objectives into reality it is necessary to form, develop, maintain and use the ability to be calm in any stressing situation.

Creative

617. Finding creative solutions that contribute to solving conflicts helps us achieve more records.

618. Finding creative solutions to the problems helps us achieve more true friendships.

619. Creative ideas help us achieve more favorable chances.

620. Finding creative solutions to the problems helps us achieve more records.

621. Finding creative solutions that contribute to solving differences helps us achieve much good luck.

622. Finding creative solutions that contribute to solving differences helps us achieve more records.

623. Finding creative solutions that contribute to solving conflicts helps us achieve more favorable chances.

624. Finding creative solutions that contribute to solving conflicts helps us achieve more favorable situations.

625. Finding creative solutions that contribute to solving conflicts helps us achieve much good luck.

626. Creative ideas help us achieve more records.

627. Finding creative solutions that contribute to solving conflicts helps us achieve more successes.

628. Creative ideas help us achieve much good luck.

629. Creative ideas help us achieve more successes.

630. Finding creative solutions to the problems helps us achieve more personal goals.

631. Finding creative solutions that contribute to solving misunderstandings helps us achieve more performances.

632. Finding creative solutions that contribute to solving differences helps us achieve more efficient co operations.

633. Creative ideas help us achieve more efficient co operations.

634. Finding creative solutions to the problems helps us achieve more pleasant surprises.

635. Finding creative solutions that contribute to solving conflicts helps us achieve more efficient co operations.

636. Finding creative solutions to the problems helps us achieve more performances.

637. Creative ideas help us achieve more true friendships.

638. Finding creative solutions that contribute to solving differences helps us achieve more successes.

639. Finding creative solutions that contribute to solving differences helps us achieve more true friendships.

640. Creative ideas help us achieve more favorable situations.

641. Finding creative solutions that contribute to solving misunderstandings helps us achieve more favorable situations.

642. Finding creative solutions that contribute to solving conflicts helps us achieve more personal goals.

643. Finding creative solutions that contribute to solving conflicts helps us achieve more pleasant surprises.

644. Finding creative solutions that contribute to solving misunderstandings helps us achieve more favorable chances.

645. Finding creative solutions to the problems helps us achieve more favorable chances.

646. Finding creative solutions to the problems helps us achieve more efficient co operations.

647. Finding creative solutions that contribute to solving differences helps us achieve more favorable situations.

648. Finding creative solutions to the problems helps us achieve more successes.

649. A great capacity of persevering until finding creative solutions helps us achieve more pleasant surprises.

650. A great capacity of persevering until finding creative solutions helps us become more understanding.

651. A great capacity of being creative in order to solve great problems must be appreciated.

652. A great capacity of being creative in order to solve great problems helps us become practical.

653. A great capacity of being creative in order to solve great problems helps us become more efficient.

654. Our resistance to changing for the better can be overcome also through the contribution of the formation, development, maintenance and usage of creative behavior.

655. A great capacity of persevering until finding creative solutions helps us achieve more favorable situations.

656. Continuous self perfection helps us become creative.

657. A great capacity of being creative in order to solve great problems must be rewarded.

658. A great capacity of persevering until finding creative solutions helps us become loving.

659. A great capacity of persevering until finding creative solutions helps us become productive.

660. A great capacity of being creative in order to solve great problems helps us become loved.

661. A great capacity of being creative in order to solve great problems helps us become productive.

662. In order to rise up once again for the first time for the who knows what time it is necessary to also form, develop, maintain and use creative behavior.

663. Pessimism can be removed and replaced with optimism also through the contribution of the formation, development, maintenance and usage of creative behavior.

664. A great capacity of being creative in order to solve great problems helps us become happier.

665. A great capacity of being creative in order to solve great problems helps us maintain our way of being loved.

666. A great capacity of persevering until finding creative solutions helps us become practical.

667. Problems cannot be solved by the ideas that created them but also through the contribution of the formation, development, maintenance and usage of creative behavior.

668. A great capacity of being creative in order to solve great problems helps us become more pleasant.

669. A great capacity of being creative in order to solve great problems helps us become more understanding.

670. A great capacity of being creative in order to solve great problems helps us achieve more efficient co operations.

671. A great capacity of persevering until finding creative solutions must be appreciated.

672. A great capacity of persevering until finding creative solutions helps us maintain our way of being liked.

673. A great capacity of persevering until finding creative solutions helps us become more efficient.

674. A great capacity of persevering until finding creative solutions helps us maintain our way of being loved.

Communication

675. Communication helps us become charming.

676. Communication helps us become initiating.

677. Communication helps us become diplomatic.

678. Communication helps us become energetic.

679. Communication helps us become daring.

680. Communication helps us become rulers.

681. Communication helps us become bold.

682. Communication helps us become strong.

683. Communication helps us become decent.

684. Communication helps us become constant.

685. Communication helps us become meticulous.

686. Communication helps us become stimulating.

687. Communication helps us become expansive.

688. Communication helps us become funny.

689. Communication helps us become loyal.

690. Communication helps us become respectful.

691. Communication helps us become confident.

692. Communication helps us become harmless.

693. Communication helps us become independent.

694. Communication helps us become sociable.

695. Communication helps us become liked.

696. Communication helps us become rigorous.

697. Communication helps us become flexible.

698. Communication helps us become decisive.

699. Communication helps us become cheerful.

700. Communication helps us become spiritual.

701. Communication helps us become profound.

702. Communication helps us become mannered.

703. Communication helps us become analytic.

704. Communication helps us become cultivated.

705. Communication helps us become popular.

706. Communication helps us become trained.

707. Communication helps us become selfless.

708. Communication helps us become convincing.

709. Communication helps us become self controlled.

710. Communication helps us become adaptable.

711. Communication helps us become animated.

712. Communication helps us become capable.

713. Communication helps us become sincere.

714. Communication helps us become positive.

715. Communication helps us become leaders.

716. Communication helps us become agreeable.

717. Communication helps us become attachable.

718. Communication helps us become good listeners.

719. Communication helps us become active.

720. Communication helps us become sure of ourselves.

721. Communication helps us become spontaneous.

722. Communication helps us become friendly.

723. Communication helps us become balanced.

724. Communication helps us become consequent.

725. Communication helps us become peacemakers.

726. Communication helps us become fighting.

727. Communication helps us become sensitive.

728. Inter-human communication sometimes helps us achieve a true love.

729. Inter-human communication sometimes helps us achieve much more true friendships.

730. Inter-human communication sometimes helps us achieve much more efficient co operations.

731. Inter-human communication sometimes helps us achieve much more performances.

732. Inter-human communication sometimes helps us achieve much more personal goals.

733. Inter-human communication sometimes helps us achieve much more successes.

734. Inter-human communication sometimes helps us achieve a happy marriage.

735. Inter-human communication sometimes helps us become more optimistic.

736. Inter-human communication sometimes helps us become wiser.

737. Inter-human communication sometimes helps us become more understanding.

738. Inter-human communication sometimes helps us become more practical.

739. Inter-human communication sometimes helps us become more pleasant.

Concentration

740. Permanent concentration on our personal objectives helps us achieve more efficient co operations.

741. Permanent concentration on our personal objectives helps us achieve more favorable situations.

742. Total concentration on personal goals helps us achieve more true friendships.

743. Permanent concentration on our personal objectives helps us achieve more pleasant surprises.

744. Total concentration on personal goals helps us achieve more performances.

745. Permanent concentration on our personal objectives helps us achieve more favorable chances.

746. Permanent concentration on our personal objectives helps us achieve more successes.

747. Total concentration on personal goals helps us achieve more pleasant surprises.

748. Permanent concentration on our personal objectives helps us achieve more personal goals.

749. Total concentration on personal goals helps us achieve more efficient co operations.

750. Total concentration on personal goals helps us achieve much good luck.

751. Permanent concentration on our personal objectives helps us achieve more performances.

752. Total concentration on personal goals helps us achieve more favorable situations.

753. Permanent concentration on our personal objectives helps us achieve much good luck.

754. Total concentration on personal goals helps us achieve more personal goals.

755. Permanent concentration on our personal objectives helps us achieve more true friendships.

756. Permanent concentration on our personal objectives helps us achieve more records.

757. Total concentration on personal goals helps us achieve more favorable chances.

758. The increased capacity of concentration of our attention helps us and contributes to increasing our efficiency in what we do.

759. To achieve quality actions to become happy and maintain our happiness, it is necessary that every time we act to focus totally on that action, to be careful in everything we do. Any little distraction can have grater or smaller negative effects on our happiness. Because of this, our happiness totally depends on our overall happiness and on the quality of actions which we achieve, on the concentration and attention with which we perform them.

760. Concentration is required and must be present in everything that we do.

Confidence

761. Confidence in the idea that we can create our luck helps us achieve more efficient co operations.

762. Confidence in the idea that we can create our luck helps us achieve more performances.

763. Confidence in the success of what we do helps us achieve more records.

764. Confidence in the success of what we do helps us achieve more efficient co operations.

765. Self confidence helps us achieve more successes.

766. Confidence in the idea that we can create our luck helps us achieve more favorable situations.

767. Confidence in the success of what we do helps us achieve more favorable chances.

768. Self confidence helps us achieve more performances.

769. Self confidence helps us achieve more true friendships.

770. Self confidence helps us achieve more pleasant surprises.

771. Confidence in the success of what we do helps us achieve more true friendships.

772. Self confidence helps us achieve more efficient co operations.

773. Confidence in the idea that we can create our luck helps us achieve more favorable chances.

774. Self confidence helps us achieve more favorable situations.

775. Self confidence helps us achieve much good luck.

776. Confidence in the success of what we do helps us achieve more successes.

777. Self confidence helps us achieve more favorable chances.

778. Confidence in the success of what we do helps us achieve much good luck.

779. Self confidence helps us achieve more records.

780. Confidence in the idea that we can create our luck helps us achieve more successes.

781. Confidence in the success of what we do helps us achieve more pleasant surprises.

782. Confidence in the idea that we can create our luck helps us achieve more records.

783. Confidence in the idea that we can create our luck helps us achieve more true friendships.

784. Confidence in the idea that we can create our luck helps us achieve more personal goals.

785. Confidence in the idea that we can create our luck helps us achieve much good luck.

786. Confidence in the success of what we do helps us achieve more favorable situations.

787. Confidence in the success of what we do helps us achieve more performances.

788. Confidence in the idea that we can create our luck helps us achieve more pleasant surprises.

789. Self confidence helps us achieve more personal goals.

790. A great capacity of increasing self confidence must be imitated.

791. A great capacity of maintaining self confidence helps us maintain our way of being loved.

792. Confidence in ourselves must be appreciated.

793. A great capacity of increasing self confidence helps us become enthusiastic.

794. A great capacity of increasing self confidence helps us become tolerant.

795. Confidence in ourselves helps us become understanding.

796. Confidence in ourselves helps us achieve much more pleasant surprises.

797. A great capacity of maintaining self confidence helps us become more productive.

798. A great capacity of maintaining self confidence helps us become understanding.

799. Confidence in ourselves helps us become energetic.

800. A great capacity of maintaining self confidence must be maintained.

801. A great capacity of maintaining self confidence helps us become more cautious.

802. Confidence in ourselves helps us become constants.

803. Confidence in ourselves helps us achieve much more performances.

804. A great capacity of increasing self confidence helps us become loved.

805. A great capacity of maintaining self confidence helps us become efficient.

806. A great capacity of increasing self confidence helps us achieve more favorable chances.

807. A great capacity of maintaining self confidence helps us achieve more efficient co operations.

808. A great capacity of increasing self confidence helps us become productive.

809. A great capacity of increasing self confidence helps us maintain our way of being cautious.

810. A great capacity of increasing self confidence helps us become more pleasant.

811. great capacity of maintaining self confidence helps us become more tolerant.

812. A great capacity of increasing self confidence helps us become practical.

813. A great capacity of maintaining self confidence helps us maintain our wisdom.

814. A great capacity of increasing self confidence helps us become happy.

815. A great capacity of increasing self confidence helps us become more practical.

816. Confidence in ourselves helps us become spiritual.

817. A great capacity of increasing self confidence must be developed.

818. A great capacity of increasing self confidence helps us maintain our efficiency.

819. A great capacity of increasing self confidence must be used.

820. A great capacity of maintaining self confidence helps us achieve more true friendships.

821. A great capacity of increasing self confidence helps us become more enthusiastic.

822. A great capacity of increasing self confidence helps us maintain our way of being practical.

823. A great capacity of increasing self confidence helps us become cautious.

824. A great capacity of increasing self confidence helps us maintain our way of being liked.

825. A great capacity of increasing self confidence must be maintained.

826. A great capacity of maintaining self confidence helps us achieve more performances.

827. A great capacity of maintaining self confidence helps us achieve more favorable situations.

828. A great capacity of maintaining self confidence helps us become happy.

829. A great capacity of maintaining self confidence helps us become more understanding.

830. Confidence in ourselves helps us achieve much more favorable chances.

831. A great capacity of increasing self confidence must be supported.

832. A great capacity of increasing self confidence helps us achieve more performances.

833. A radical transformation for the better of our life can be achieved also through the

contribution of the formation, development, maintenance and usage of the greater ability to have confidence in ourselves.

834. In order to change the desire of changing into reality it is necessary to form, develop, maintain and use the ability to have confidence in yourself.

835. The sense of achieving quality in everything we do increases our confidence in ourselves.

836. Persons with human social behaviors have more confidence in the future.

837. People who have not succeeded in obtaining a happy marriage must develop their confidence in themselves.

838. Those without hopes for the future need to become friends with those who have confidence in themselves.

839. Efficient people in positive actions have more chances to develop their confidence in the future.

840. Those who know how to take advantage of the opportunity of creation increase their confidence in themselves.

841. The sense of achievement and quality in everything we do develops our confidence in the future.

842. Confidence in ourselves helps us a lot to achieve more and greater successes.

843. Self confidence increases our possibilities to achieve efficient co-developments.

844. Those willing to try new ways increase their confidence in themselves through achievements.

845. Our corresponding conception of life contributes to increasing our confidence in ourselves.

846. True friendships increase our confidence in ourselves.

847. A man with a good imagination of himself has a greater confidence in himself.

848. Those who know that discipline is one of the keys of dreams increase their confidence in themselves.

849. Those who discover unique ways to work efficiently for a better life increase their confidence in themselves.

850. Those who solve problems only through constructive methods have a greater confidence in themselves.

851. Those who have opportunities to develop have more chances to increase their confidence in themselves.

852. The sense of organization helps and contributes to increasing our confidence in ourselves.

853. Those with the sense of responsibility have a higher confidence in themselves.

854. Most women and men are looking for a happy marriage, but unfortunately they do too little, give too little time, too little attention to that and to achieving and maintaining it. If on the contrary, they will do what is necessary to achieve and maintain a happy marriage, they will surely achieve it. I wish you success with the confidence that you will be able to achieve and maintain a happy marriage. Good luck again.

855. The more experience we have to help us achieve our personal goals, the more confidence we have in a better future.

Anger

856. The self-control of our behaviors helps us a lot to prevent anger.

857. People who have had successes have known how to cope with many dangers.

858. Those who have high objectives in life know how to overcome the dangers that come in life most of the times.

859. The quality of sensing situations helps us a lot to avoid dangers.

860. Political corruption is a very great danger to democracy.

861. The quality of sensing situations helps us a lot to discover danger.

862. In anger many words are said that, after they are said, people who said them regret it.

863. The state of anger makes us commit more mistakes.

864. The state of anger makes it very hard for us to achieve our desired future.

865. The state of anger prevents us from having more chances to meet more favorable situations.

866. The state of anger stops us from finding the right partner in life.

867. The state of anger makes achieving the greater good a lot harder.

868. The state of anger makes maintaining true friendships more difficult.

869. The state of anger makes achieving a mature love more difficult.

870. The state of anger is bad for our health.

871. Anger is a primitive very harmful behavior.

872. In anger many disastrous arguments can be caused.

873. In anger many harmful offenses can be made.

874. In anger many true friendships can be broken.

875. In anger many words are said that are not supposed to be said.

876. In anger many unfixable mistakes can be made.

877. Human stupidity is incredibly dangerous most of the times.

878. The state of anger makes it hard for us to achieve success.

879. The state of anger makes it hard for us to achieve our personal goals.

880. The state of anger can cause many accidents.

881. Corrupt politicians are very dangerous; they are like viruses.

882. The man that you can not trust is dangerous.

883. A lying man is extremely dangerous.

884. aziness is a dangerous defect.

885. Laziness a dangerous defect.

886. A man who is careless and without objectives is a danger to himself.

887. A man who is careless about himself and about others is dangerous.

888. The man who is irrational is extremely dangerous.

889. Boorishness is an extremely dangerous flaw.

890. The man who does not even know what is good for him is extremely dangerous.

891. Anger is an incorrect behavior with multiple negative effects.

892. Anger harms a happy marriage.

893. Anger harms our health.

894. Anger creates stress to that who is angry.

895. Repeated and extended anger creates more stress.

896. Repeated and extended anger harms our health very much.

897. Anger is a primitive behavior.

898. Anger has only negative effects.

899. Hypocrisy is extremely dangerous.

900. The man who is sick is extremely dangerous.

901. Artfulness is a very dangerous flaw.

902. The foolish man is extremely dangerous.

903. He who is irrational is extremely dangerous.

904. Discrimination is a very dangerous factor of stress.

905. Envy is a cancer, very dangerous, it eats us on the inside.

906. Anger greatly harms many times even the one who manifests it.

907. Waste is extremely dangerous.

908. Pettiness is extremely dangerous.

909. Stupidity is extremely dangerous.

910. A man without judgement is extremely dangerous.

911. Revenge is extremely dangerous.

912. Hatred is extremely dangerous.

913. The man whom you can not trust is dangerous.

914. Corruption is so generalized in the world and so harmful that it constitutes a global danger of humanity, the greatest and the most dangerous and with negative effects that it creates for society.

915. Organized state crime is the most dangerous crime because it is conducted by officials of state and elected officials, other staff working for the state or on behalf of the state and they are using their function in avhieving the crime of using their function, institution and other institutions of the state.

916. Dehumanization is very dangerous to society.

917. The one who is quick in anger complicates many problems.

918. The one who is quick in anger creates many problems.

919. The one who is quick in anger creates many conflicts.

920. The one who is quick in anger makes many mistakes.

921. The one who is quick in anger does himself much harm.

922. Anger does not resolve problems.

923. Anger can be prevented by thinking positive.

924. Anger harms us always.

925. Anger has created many misfortunes.

926. Anger makes us make mistakes.

927. Anger makes us think wrongly.

Conflicts

928. Finding creative solutions that contribute to solving conflicts helps us achieve more records.

929. Preventing conflicts helps us achieve more personal goals.

930. Preventing conflicts helps us achieve more favorable chances.

931. The ability to solve conflicts helps us achieve more successes.

932. Preventing conflicts helps us achieve more successes.

933. Finding creative solutions that contribute to solving conflicts helps us achieve more favorable chances.

934. Finding creative solutions that contribute to solving conflicts helps us achieve more favorable situations.

935. Finding creative solutions that contribute to solving conflicts helps us achieve much good luck.

936. The ability to solve conflicts helps us achieve more favorable situations.

937. The art of solving conflicts helps us achieve more performances.

938. The ability to solve conflicts helps us achieve more pleasant surprises.

939. Preventing conflicts helps us achieve more true friendships.

940. Finding creative solutions that contribute to solving conflicts helps us achieve more successes.

941. The art of solving conflicts helps us achieve more true friendships.

942. The ability to solve conflicts helps us achieve much good luck.

943. The ability to solve conflicts helps us achieve more records.

944. The art of solving conflicts helps us achieve more records.

945. The ability to solve conflicts helps us achieve more efficient co operations.

946. Preventing conflicts helps us achieve much good luck.

947. Finding creative solutions that contribute to solving conflicts helps us achieve more efficient co operations.

948. The art of solving conflicts helps us achieve more successes.

949. The art of solving conflicts helps us achieve more personal goals.

950. The art of solving conflicts helps us achieve more pleasant surprises.

951. Finding creative solutions that contribute to solving conflicts helps us achieve more personal goals.

952. The art of solving conflicts helps us achieve more efficient co operations.

953. The ability to solve conflicts helps us achieve more true friendships.

954. Preventing conflicts helps us achieve more favorable situations.

955. Preventing conflicts helps us achieve more records.

956. Preventing conflicts helps us achieve more performances.

957. The art of solving conflicts helps us achieve more favorable chances.

958. Finding creative solutions that contribute to solving conflicts helps us achieve more performances.

959. Preventing conflicts helps us achieve more efficient co operations.

960. The ability to solve conflicts helps us achieve more performances.

961. The art of solving conflicts helps us achieve much good luck.

962. The ability to solve conflicts helps us achieve more personal goals.

963. Finding creative solutions that contribute to solving conflicts helps us achieve more true friendships.

964. The art of solving conflicts helps us achieve more favorable situations.

965. The ability to solve conflicts helps us achieve more favorable chances.

966. Finding creative solutions that contribute to solving conflicts helps us achieve more pleasant surprises.

967. Life is much more beautiful in a marriage when there are no conflicts between spouses.

968. By developing their inner beauty, women also develop their abilities that can help them prevent certain conflicts.

969. The self-control of our behaviors helps us a lot to prevent some conflicts.

970. A vigilant man has more chances to prevent more conflicts.

971. Knowing ourselves helps us a lot to prevent many conflicts.

972. Conflicts can be avoided most of the times.

973. Continuous conflicts are bad for our health.

974. Conflicts can be prevented.

975. By preventing the formation of causes of conflicts we can prevent the apparition of conflicts.

976. Positive imagination helps us prevent many conflicts.

977. Common values help us a lot to prevent many conflicts.

978. Positive ideas prevent many potential conflicts.

979. People who are calm in any situation prevent many conflicts.

980. Our responsibility helps us prevent many possible conflicts.

981. Positive actions prevent many conflicts.

982. A realistic man in interpersonal relations has greater chances to avoid many conflicts.

983. People who are calm in any situation have many chances to prevent many conflicts.

984. Unresolved conflicts at the workplace lead to resignations, transfers, annulments of work contracts, etc.

985. People who have everything know how to prevent many conflicts.

986. The quality of sensing situations helps us prevent conflicts.

987. An agile man knows how to prevent conflicts.

988. The greater good prevents many conflicts.

989. Humanist global cooperation contributes a lot in reducing the number of armed and unarmed conflicts.

990. Efficient global co operations will prevent many possible conflicts.

991. Discipline prevents conflicts.

992. Humanist economy can reduce sufferings, troubles, accidents, conflicts, negative effects of actions a lot.

993. Humanist economy would lead to preventing many international conflicts and wars.

994. Respecting the right to nondiscrimination of people contributes a lot to preventing many conflicts.

995. Self- control prevents many conflicts

996. Common values prevent conflicts.

997. Responsibility prevents conflicts.

998. Cooperation prevents many conflicts.

999. Co-development prevents many conflicts.

1000.Each of us has had one or more bigger or smaller failures. It's good not to have any failures or as few failures as possible. Some or more failures could harm us very much. Those who were careful did not achieve failure or failures and have made smaller, fewer ones. Prevision helps us prevent many failures. The more experienced in previsioning we are, the greater ability we have to provide, as we have more knowledge necessary to achieve previsions etc.. the more we can make accurate previsions, prevent many mistakes, failures, trouble, accidents, conflicts, arguments, unsuccessful actions, etc. In our personal and professional life, it is necessary to continuously develop and to have that personal goal to develop to a maximum capacity the prevision in private life, the ability to use previsions. We can continuously increase the capacity of our prevision very much, as we live if we have personal objectives, as we expand our ability to prevision and whether we act to continuously and effectively achieve this objective. Those who aimed at personal living as to develop the capacity of prevision continuously and concretely act with dedication to achieve their capacity to make a prevision which will help them achieve one or more very big successes, they will succeed to prevent many failures, troubles, etc., they will be able to achieve much in life, to have many happy, satisfying moments and so much happiness. The more we have a capacity of more than prevision, a more accurate, more efficient one, the more valuable we are for having this treasure. This treasure we can continuously increase greatly. The capacity of prevision generally contains more capacities of prevision in some actions, behaviors in the achievement of personal objectives, private, professional, specific ones, etc. It is necessary to develop those capabilities specific to prediction that we need. Knowledge, experience, qualifications, skills, etc., in a specific prevision capacity can be used to a greater or lesser degree in other capacities specific to prevision. The capacities of prevision are very necessary and very useful to us but unfortunately very few people have personal goals in life to continuously develop the specific performance of prevision. Due to the special importance of the capacity of prevision it is necessary and required to create and develop the science of the development of the capacity of prevision, because having this science we would have it by applying enormous positive effects on countless people that should develop and apply it indirectly on other people. The state would accelerate progress in many fields, would accelerate the reduction of illiteracy, poverty, illness, divorces out of arguments and conflict, accidents, what harms humans, animals, the environment, etc.. It would lead to solving many personal and state targets, it would create enormously many joys, much satisfaction and happiness. It would lead to the situation that most people no longer live at the whim of chance, with no personal, professional security, etc.. but on the contrary they would lead to more people having them as an objective and as they continue to live, they would develop the personal capacities necessary for their prevision and apply them every day, both in the establishment of private personal or professional life, it would be something concrete that will help them achieve more harmonious lives to achieve what they want and need for their families. There is the capacity of prevision in specific persons, specific societies, specific legal entities, nonprofit organizations, companies, banks, groups, collectivities, international and intergovernmental organizations. Both individuals and legal entities, must not live from hand to mouth, must act firmly, must study and evaluate the effects of positive and negative actions, decisions, etc. their objectives are also necessary to be: 1) to aim at continuing to develop their capacities of specific prediction that they need, 2) to apply, continuous use in any action, situation-specific prediction capabilities necessary and useful efforts, energy consumption and costs for the development and capacity of specific prevision that they need.

Failures can happen in each of our actions or less often. Our failures can be created by factors and actions sometimes difficult to identify and prevent. However there are actions where we can know all the factors that can create failures. Knowing the factors that create failures in actions, we can take the necessary measures to prevent them by reaching in some cases to zero failures, as they have succeeded in situations in a long time, in many states, especially people in the most developed countries of the world. How to develop more this science with the more than we can know more of the factors that could cause failures in certain situations to certain actions. Scientific knowledge can contribute greatly to preventing many failures in many actions. At present people do not use scientific knowledge, the human experience gained in books, studies, on the Internet, although they have committed enormously many failures, mistakes, although they could prevent many huge mistakes, failures if they would use efficient, organized, timely human experience and knowledge from books, the Internet when they would need it. Countries should take immediate measures and be more interested in people and use them when they need knowledge and human experience that can reach and can be used. Human knowledge is growing and increases daily awfully much, and human experience which can create the situation so that we can prevent every day more even more mistakes and failures with positive effects on our high society, to accelerate progress in many areas.

Where we have failures we should never discourage and lose our wits, our balance inside, our optimism, morale or to start to grieve. If we do this, it would solve absolutely no problem, but on the contrary, it would stress us illogically, abnormally without any positive effects. Those who have achieved many successes knew how to cope with failure, learning from failures, to reduce the negative effects of failures. Many failures rather than strengthening us, they weaken us, they should give us power instead of imobilizing us and mobilize us instead of making them harder to give motivation, instead of multiple negative effects they should have have multiple positive effects.

However, I disagree and do not consider as logical, positive or constructive the popular saying: „Man learns from mistakes". Man, on the contrary should learn only from his successes and from those who have achieved successes and gained, by imitating those positive behaviors, which have effectively contributed to success. In addition man can learn enormously not to have failures, or make mistakes from the knowledge and positive experience of mankind stored in books, media, on the Internet and the experience of people who have huge experience and knowledge. The more we can prevent more failures, mistakes, the more we can prevent more and more different negative effects. It would be necessary and useful the development of a science to prevent human errors because it would prevent a large number of human errors and failures if people study and apply it as much and in as many actions as they can. This knowledge could and should be studied in colleges and universities and other educational forms. In every area of activity for each action type, it could identify factors that create human mistakes and failures and then it could identify solutions and measures to be taken to prevent mistakes and failures. Efforts and expenses that will be done by creating, developing, learning and applicating the science to prevent human errors will not be much lower than the positive effects of their prevention of a very large number of mistakes and failures and their multiple, diverse and very large negative effects. Financial investment, energy, time, etc.. in these activities related to the prevention of human errors and failures would be very effective and necessary and useful for both countries and for people in particular. Each of us in a greater or lesser way can participate in the creation, development and application of the science to prevent human errors.

1001. Routine is very necessary and useful in behavior, etc. in actions for a certain period of time. After a certain period of time, at a certain time it is necessary to get rid of a certain routine, a certain behavior, a way of thinking, a certain kind of action, etc.. and replace it with another behavior more efficiently, more operational, more tactful, more thoughtful, etc.. in order to progress in achieving what we proposed, our personal objectives. When we need to get rid, to escape a certain routine it is necessary to get rid of it immediately, without doubts, delay, fears, etc. and to act in the new action, new behavior more effectively, without any delay. People who have the ability to leave a certain routine immediately when they need to, progress much faster in life, carry out much faster and more efficient personal goals, performe in live many more bigger or smaller successes than those who do not get rid of a particular or specific routine when necessary. Routine, when we get rid of it when necessary is a big negative factor of progress, it creates many failures, misfortunes, difficulties in achieving personal goals in life, it creates misunderstandings in families and may even lead to divorce, misunderstandings and even conflicts between large generations etc.. The routine of a normal fact, when we can not get rid of it, and it is necessary to get rid of it, it may actually become a very harmful fact for our new family, for the people around, for society, for younger generations and for the future, it may sometimes have many negative effects, very large and very diverse ones. For these reasons it is necessary to continuously develop our ability to get rid of routine when needed immediately.

1002. Those who have had a negative thinking in certain situations had many troubles, failures, conflicts in the family, some came to divorce, and they have achieved little success too.

1003. When we think constructively not destructively, we think this helps us prevent many mistakes, failures, accidents, divorces, misfortunes, conflicts, which are bad, harmful to us or others.

1004. Mental self-development is of enormous help in preventing a lot of failures, sorrows, mistakes, illnesses, accidents, conflicts, arguments, divorces, negative actions, inefficiencies, etc.

1005. If each of us would be more unselfish on this earth there would be much more happiness, more joy and satisfactions, much more prosperity, harmony, understanding, more goodness, and much less trouble, misery, misfortune, accidents, diseases, illnesses, illiteracy, poverty, etc. Therefore each of us could and should be more unselfish in as many situations as possible. Acts of selflessness from each of us should lead step by step to creating a safer world with fewer conflicts, wars, acts of terrorism etc.

1006. Consensus is a situation that prevents many conflicts, trouble, divisive, arguments, loss of time etc..

1007. Forethought is a quality that is required of each spouse in the family. Only with forethought a husband and wife can avoid many potential trouble, failures, conflicts, etc. in marriage.

1008. Caution in marriage helps us enormously to avoid conflicts, arguments, hate, distrust and sometimes even divorce. The more each of the spouses is cautious the better it is.

1009. Abstention is a quality, a behavior that is necessary for both spouses to have because abstention in situations that require the prevention of conflicts, they worsen the negative conflicts, quarrels, misunderstandings, disputes of marriage and sometimes even marriage itself.

1010. The tact of each spouse enormously helps them prevent many conflicts, arguments, misunderstandings, dispute and even divorce.

1011. Each of the spouses need to always be calculated in family relations in order to prevent arguments, conflicts, misunderstandings etc..

1012. When respect disappears between spouses in a family, disputes arise, conflicts, arguments, mistrust and ultimately it is very likely in many families for divorce to occur.

1013. Those with tact succeed in avoiding misunderstandings, conflicts, arguments, annoyances within the family.

1014. Arrogance leads to many conflicts.

1015. Totalitarianism creates conflicts.

1016. One's self-control prevents many conflicts.

1017. The one who is quick in anger creates many conflicts.

1018. Non-discrimination prevents many conflicts.

Correct

1019. Our chances of becoming happy increase if we establish our personal goals correctly.

1020. Our chances of becoming happy increase if we plan our actions correctly.

1021. Our chances of becoming happy increase if we are correctly organize.

1022. Successes in life can also be achieved thanks to the correct establishment of our personal goals.

1023. Our way of seeing family relations, if it is correct helps us a lot to achieve a happy marriage.

1024. Our way of seeing family relations can be correct or incorrect.

1025. Our way of seeing love relations, if it is incorrect stops the achievement of true love.

1026. Our way of seeing love relations, if it is correct helps us a lot to achieve a true love.

1027. Our way of seeing love relations can be correct or incorrect.

1028. Correct appreciations are appreciated a lot.

1029. He who makes correct appreciations is esteemed by people.

1030. He who makes correct appreciations is appreciated a lot by people.

1031. People want to be appreciated correctly.

1032. Illegal accusations can be prevented by effective laws and their correct application.

1033. Mutual correct appreciations maintain friendships.

1034. Those who see life in an incorrect way have a lot to suffer in life.

1035. When we see life in an incorrect way it harms us a lot.

1036. Developing our thinking can be achieved also through the formation, development, maintenance and usage of a correct life conception.

1037. We can become stronger and we cannot let ourselves be influenced by the world also through the contribution of the formation, development, maintenance and usage of a correct life conception.

1038. Correct thinking can be formed, developed and used also through the contribution of the formation, development, maintenance and usage of all only objective ideas.

1039. Forming vices can be prevented also through the contribution of the formation, development, maintenance and usage of correct behaviors.

1040. We can replace wrong ideas with correct ideas also through the contribution of the formation, development, maintenance and usage of efficient ideas.

1041. Stress can be prevented also through the contribution of the formation, development, maintenance and usage of correct behaviors.

1042. Emancipation from restrictions can be achieved if we use our time correctly.

1043. We can make correct decisions if we know ourselves.

1044. In order not to let ourselves be overwhelmed by the difficulties of life it is necessary to form, develop, maintain and use a correct life conception.

1045. Forming wrong ideas can be prevented through the contribution of the formation, development, maintenance and usage of correct thinking.

1046. Emancipation from restrictions can be made through the formation, development, maintenance and usage of correct thinking.

1047. We can prevent the falling apart of a happy marriage also through the contribution of the formation, development, maintenance and usage of correct behaviors.

1048. Pessimism can be removed through the contribution of the formation, development, maintenance and usage of correct thinking.

1049. A correct thinking can be formed by using logical thinking.

1050. We can replace wrong ideas with correct ideas through finding and using correct ideas.

1051. The meaning of life can be found through the contribution of the formation, development, maintenance and usage of correct ideas.

1052. Our own personality can be maintained through the correct decisions we make.

1053. Forming around ideas can be prevented through the contribution of the formation, development, maintenance and usage of correct ideas.

1054. Efficient ideas are always correct ideas.

1055. We can replace wrong ideas with correct ideas through using normal ideas.

1056. Forming wrong ideas can be prevented also through the formation, development, maintenance and usage of correct ideas.

1057. Problems cannot be solved by the ideas that created them but through the contribution of the formation, development, maintenance and usage of correct thinking.

1058. In order to take correct decisions it is necessary that we form, develop, maintain and use the ability to be responsible.

1059. Problems cannot be solved by the ideas that created them but by other ideas and also through the contribution of the formation, development, maintenance and usage of correct thinking.

1060. We can replace wrong ideas with correct ideas also through the contribution of the formation, development, maintenance and usage of correct ideas.

1061. We can overcome the difficulties that we must surpass also through the formation, development and maintenance of correct thinking.

1062. Emancipation from self imposed restrictions can be made through the formation, development and maintenance of correct thinking.

1063. In order to prevent not achieving our personal goals we need to form, develop, maintain and use only correct ideas.

1064. Desperation can be eliminated also through the contribution of the formation, development, maintenance and usage of a correct conception of life.

1065. Developing our thinking can be achieved also through the formation, development, maintenance and usage of only correct ideas.

1066. In order to take correct decisions we need to form, develop, maintain and use the ability to solve problems legally.

1067. We can distinguish right from wrong better and faster also through the contribution of the formation, development, maintenance and usage of correct thinking.

1068.We can replace wrong ideas where correct ideas also through the contribution of the formation, development, maintenance and usage of the ability to use positive ideas.

1069.In order to escape poverty it is necessary to form, develop, maintain and use correct thinking.

1070.In order to change our desire of changing it is a really necessary that we form, develop, maintain and use correct thinking.

1071.In order to pursue and transform our personal goals into reality we need to form, develop, maintain and use correct thinking as well.

1072.Forming wrong ideas can be prevented also through the formation, development, maintenance and usage of the ability to select correct ideas from wrong ideas.

1073.Forming the wrong ideas about what is happening to us can be prevented also through the contribution of the formation, development, maintenance and usage of correct thinking.

1074. Our happiness depends a lot on the formation, development, maintenance and usage of the ability to constantly choose correctly.

1075. In order to take corrective decisions it is necessary to form, develop, maintain and use the ability to react with understanding.

1076. The solutions to the problems we have we can find also through the contribution of the formation, development, maintenance and usage of correct thinking.

1077. We can replace wrong ideas with correct ideas also through the contribution of the formation, development, maintenance and usage of responsible ideas.

1078. Preventing the formation of doubts can also be achieved through the formation, development, maintenance and usage of correct thinking.

1079. We can replace wrong ideas with correct ideas also through the contribution of the formation, development, maintenance and usage of an optimistic conception of life.

1080. We can replace wrong ideas with correct ideas also through the contribution of the formation, development, maintenance and usage of a constructive conception of life.

1081. We can replace wrong ideas with the correct ideas also through the contribution of the formation, development, maintenance and usage of a positive life conception.

1082. In order to pursue and transform our personal goals into reality we need to form and develop correct thinking.

1083. Preventing stress can be achieved also through the contribution of the formation, development, maintenance and usage of a correct behavior.

1084. Correct thinking can be formed, developed, maintained and used also through the contribution of the formation, development, maintenance and usage of correct ideas.

1085. We can replace wrong ideas with correct ideas also through the contribution of the formation, development, maintenance and usage of constructive ideas.

1086. The desire to make others happy can be achieved through the contribution of the formation, development, maintenance and usage of correct thinking.

Character

1087. Sometimes luck appears only because we have a character.

1088. People who have had successes are people of character.

1089. A responsible man is also a man of character.

1090. A man's character can create many riches, but riches can not give back the character if it is lost.

1091. Those who have as a personal objective the harmonious development of their character will succeed in life and achieve a more beautiful life than those who do not have among their personal goals the harmonious development of their personality.

1092. Those who have as a personal objective the harmonious development of their character will succeed in life to achieve more successes and far fewer failures than those who do not have personal objectives and do not target their own harmonious development of their personality.

1093. The man who has no good sense has no character.

1094. Moral wealth is given by the moral character and values that each of us has.

Credibility

1095. Moral values continuously increase our credibility.

1096. Solving problems through positive methods increases our credibility.

1097. Those who discover unique ways to work efficiently for a better life increase their credibility.

1098. A positive conception of life increases our credibility.

1099. Long term thinking increases our credibility.

1100. Constructive thinking increases our credibility.

1101. Those who control circumstances increase their credibility.

1102. Those who willingly expand their positive experience increase their credibility.

1103. Efficient people in positive actions have more chances of increasing their credibility.

1104. Those who know that discipline is one of the keys of dreams increased their credibility.

1105. The sense of objectivity increases the credibility of the person who has it.

1106. Sometimes the lack of common sense enormously reduces the credibility of the ones who do not have common sense.

1107. Concentrating our energies increases our credibility.

1108. A non hostile but aggressive behavior helps us increase our credibility.

1109. People who are resistant to stress have a greater credibility.

1110. Credibility many times brings us luck.

1111. A positive enterprising spirit increases our credibility.

1112. The sense of credibility helps us become more credible.

1113. The sense of fairness increases our credibility.

1114. Those who know how to take advantage of the opportunity to create increase their credibility.

1115. Solving problems only through constructive methods increases our credibility.

Biography

Cornel Gheorghe Ardelean was born on March 11.1954 in place Macea, Arad Country Romania Graduate of Economic University, Craiova Romania

1979-1989 Economist and Chief Economist and sales Department

In 1990-founding member of the first Parliament of Romania after the Revolution of 1989 in PCNU (Provisional Council of National Unity)

1992 - Independent candidate for deputy in the Romanian Parliament, Chamber of Deputies

1992-1996 Advisor to the Arad Country Council as an independent adviser

1992-1996 President of the Commission trade, tourism, services advise Arad Country Council

1990-2002 Director, manager of private companies wholesale

1980 - Philosopher and author books.

1980 He published 118 books, articles in publications, of which 50 English books and 68 books in Romanian

In 2009 - Member and Coordinator of Department programs, projects and activities of the non-profit .International Organisation Cornel Gheorghe Ardelean (OIAGC)

As a thought on long-term, positive, constructive, open, creative, humanistic, etc. It has a great ability to create so many positive ideas and solutions, constructive, humanist, creative, helpful people to achieve what they want. Thinking and ideas sustain and promote the rights of children, women, all people in the world, positive thinking and ideas, constructive, humanistic, tolerante, progressive, understanding and peace between peoples and nations.